GUSTOS Y DISGUSTOS SON NO MAS QUE IMAGINACION

To Barbara,
with great affection,
Claudio

Pedro Calderón de la Barca

GUSTOS Y DISGUSTOS SON NO MAS QUE IMAGINACION

Estudio y edición crítica, por
CLAUDIO Y. SILVA
San José State University

COLECCION PLAZA MAYOR SCHOLAR

PLAYOR, S. A.  MADRID

Depósito Legal: 17853-1974
I S B N 84-359-0161-0
P L A Y O R , S . A .
Apartado 50.869, MADRID
Printed in Spain
Impreso en España

P L A Y O R , S . A . - Mar Menor, 16 - MADRID-33

To my parents
JUAN AND ANDREA SILVA

TABLE OF CONTENTS

PREFACE

An outstanding factor makes of Gustos y disgustos son no más que imaginación *an extraordinary* comedia. *It develops a medieval Spanish legend into an intriguing drama that contains all the ingredients of a poignant, seventeenth-century tragedy, yet it ends happily.*

The present study has two principal objectives: to present a critical edition of the play and to make a detailed analysis of its structure from the standpoint of theme, characterization, versification, and technique, thus offering a critical judgment of the merits of a relatively obscure work by a luminary of Spanish Golden Age drama.

Part I includes a description of the earliest known publication, discusses the editions and performances of the play, presents a study of the origins of the legend which serves as point of departure for the plot (the troubled marriage of Don Pedro II of Aragon and Doña María of Montpellier), traces the development of the legend through early chronicles, a ballad, and the works of other writers predating Calderón, and presents an analysis of the play.

Part II consists of the annotated text of the play, based on the first known printed edition of 1657. (All subsequent editions have been based on the Vera Tassis version of 1694, repeating the arbitrary additions and omissions of Vera Tassis.) The present compilation represents the first attempt at a critical edition of Gustos y disgustos.

Part III is composed of the notes to the text and the list of variants found in collating the texts of 1657 and 1694.

I wish to express my gratitude to Professor Everett W. Hesse, eminent scholar of Spanish Golden Age literature at the University of Maryland, for his inspiration in the initial stages of the preparation of this study. I also wish to thank Professors Roberto Jorge Dodson-Domínguez of Saint Gregory's College and Dorothy McMahon of the University of Southern California for their generous interest and counsel.

PART 1
INTRODUCTION

CHAPTER I

THE PLAY AND ITS EDITIONS

An original manuscript of *Gustos y disgustos son no más que imaginación* by Pedro Calderón de la Barca does not exist. Harry Hilborn, basing his opinion on very careful studies pertaining to the metric forms which predominate in the various periods of Calderón's career, places the approximate date of *Gustos y disgustos* at 1634. [1] The earliest publication date of which there is any record is 1657 when the play was included in a collection with the title of *Comedias nuevas escogidas de los mejores ingenios de España.* This collection consisted af twelve plays written by Calderón, Coello, Moreto, Mira de Amescua, Álvaro Cubillo, Rodrigo de Herrera, and Lope de Vega. *Gustos y disgustos* is the fourth *comedia* in order. There

---

[1] Harry W. HILBORN, *A Chronology of the Plays of Don Pedro Calderón de la Barca* (Toronto: University of Toronto Press, 1938), pp. 20-34.

are two printings of this edition, both bearing the same date, the text of both being identical in every respect. One edition, obtained in microfilm from the Biblioteca Nacional of Madrid, is catalogued under the number R.22.661. The title page for the entire volume contains the following information: Comedias / Nuevas / Escogidas de los / Meiores Ingenios / De España. / Octava Parte. / Dedicadas / A. D. Iuan de Luján y Aragón, Cauallero del / Orden de Santiago. / Año (the coat of arms of the *Mecenas)* 1657. / Plieg. 66° / Con privilegio. / En Madrid. Por Andrés García de la Iglesia. / A Costa de Iuan de S. Vicente, Mercader de libros. Véndese en su casa en la / calle Mayor, en frente de las Gradas de San Felipe.

The backside of the title page is blank. Page two contains the dedication of San Vicente, extending into the backside of the same page with no date. In the dedication, San Vicente reminds Luján that in the year 1653 he had dedicated another collection of plays to him-the *parte V*. Page three contains the «Licencia del Ordinario.» On the backside of this page are found the permission of Padre Niseno: Madrid, October 16, 1656 and that of Padre Jerónimo de Salcedo, November 1, 1656. The latter states that the plays of the volume had been performed and some of them had been previously published. Page four contains the «Suma del Privilegio» to San Vicente for a period of ten years. It is dated in Madrid, December 4, 1656. The «Fe de Erratas» is dated January 29, 1657 and is signed by Carlos Murcia de la Llana. The «Suma de la Tassa» follows, stating that the book is taxed at four *maravedís* a folio, «el qual tiene sesenta y cinco pliegos, y medio sin principios, ni tablas; que a este precio monta docientos y sesenta y dos maravedís»; it is dated in Madrid, February 1, 1657. On the backside is the table of contents giving the titles of the *comedias* contained in the book. No separate preliminaries are provided for each play in the collection.

The other publication of the same date, obtained in microfilm from Boston Public Library (catalogue number D. 172.1 V.8), is identical to the one just described-the only exception being that the title page differs considerably. On this title page the following information appears: Comedias / Nuevas / Escogidas de los / Mejores Ingenios de España /[2] Parte 8 /[3] Octaba.[4] Don Franco de Ansalda.[5] / Con Licencia. En Madrid.

Folio 82 erroneously reads 28 —this discrepancy is not found in the other publication of the same date. In describing this edition, Emilio Cotarelo y Mori,[6] oddly enough, gives an exact description of the *portada* containing the coat of arms of the *Mecenas*, but makes note of the error in foliation which occurs in the other publication.

Since he gave descriptions of two different books, it must be assumed that Cotarelo y Mori was familiar with both publications. What is puzzling is that he should not make mention of this fact.

The first of the two publications just described has been selected as the *princeps* edition for this study. In making this selection two factors were taken into consideration. First, the publication containing the most

---

[2] «España» appears slightly blurred with indications of the word having been superimposed over the previous impression which did not turn out clear enough.

[3] The word «Octava» was scratched out and a very untidy Arabic numeral eight was scribbled above.

[4] Written underneath «Parte» in a very poor hand.

[5] The top part of a stylized design of a bouquet of flowers in a basket separates the first and second elements of the name.

[6] *Catálogo descriptivo de la gran colección de comedias escogidas que consta de cuarenta y ocho volúmenes, impresos de 1652 a 1704* (Madrid: Tip. de Archivos, 1932), p. 45.

complete information on the title page (and more closely conforming to the description given by Cotarelo y Mori) was deemed to be more apt to be the original edition. Second, the fact that the error in foliation would occur in the other publication lent evidence to the belief that it had been a hastily prepared edition printed from the borrowed plates of the authentic first publication.

In 1682 Juan de Vera Tassis y Villarroel included *Gustos y disgustos* in the *Verdadera quinta parte de comedias de don Pedro Calderón de la Barca.* The tenth play in order is *Gustos y disgustos.* Two identical reprints of this *parte* followed in 1694 and 1730. Since all subsequent editions of the play were based on the Vera Tassis version, collating the Vera Tassis edition with the *princeps* is sufficient comparison for this study.

The 1694 edition obtained in microfilm from the Biblioteca Nacional of Madrid (catalogue number R.11.345), is the one collated with the *princeps* edition. On the title page of the *Verdadera quinta parte* appears the following information: Verdadera / Quinta Parte / de / Comedias /de Don Pedro Calderon / de la Barca, / Cavallero del Orden de Santiago, / Capellan de Honor de su Magestad, y de los / señores Reyes Nuevos de la Santa Iglesia / de la Ciudad de Toledo, celebre / Poeta Español. / Que Publica. / Don Juan de Vera Tassis / y Villarroel Chronista de Su Magestad en estos / Reynos de Castilla, y Leon, y Fiscal de las / Comedias de España. / Con Privilegio: / en Madrid: Por Francisco Sanz, Impressor del Reyno, y Portero / de Camara de Su Magestad, Año de 1694.

Photographic copies of the title pages of the *princeps* and the Vera Tassis editions follow this page. In the course of this study the *princeps* edition and the Vera Tassis edition will be referred to as P and VT respectively.

COMEDIAS NVEVAS ESCOGIDAS DE LOS MEIORES INGENIOS DE ESPANA.

OCTAVA PARTE.

DEDICADAS

A D. Iuan de Luján y Aragon, Cauallero del Orden de Santiago.

Año 1657.

Plieg. 66.

CON PRIVILEGIO.

EN MADRID. Por Andres Garcia de la Iglesia.
A costa de Iuan de S. Vicente, Mercader de libros. Vendese en su casa en la calle Mayor, enfrente de las gradas de san Felipe.

Iesus, esparciendo arroyos
como de corales finos.
Mandè luego abrir las puertas
de aquesta sala, aduertido
de lo que tu me mandaste,
y las primeras que vimos
entrar fueron dos mugeres,
que despues de auer teñido
los rostros con sangre suya,
destrançados y esparcidos
por el rostro los cabellos,
con lamentos, y con gritos,
desalentando los pechos,
y animando los suspiros,
rendidas a los desmayos,
quedaron sobre el suplicio
con los cabellos cubiertos
los rostros, que en sangre tintos,
para darnos mayor pena,
nos parecieron mas lindos.

S. le Don Sancho:

D S. B. Aqui estoy, señor,

Duq. Don Sancho,
este exemplo muerto, y viuo
mirad, y tened paciencia.

D. S. B. Ay señor! con que cuchillo
tan riguroso me has muerto!
Ay don Sancho! Ay hijo mio!

D q. Vn padre que crio mal
a su hijo mal preuisto,
aplaudiendo trauesuras,
y complaciendo delitos.
Y dos mugeres, que fueron
causa de sus excessiuos
delitos, el cielo justo
piadosamente ha querido
que le señalen la culpa,
y le adornen el suplicio,
porque assi acabe la historia
del exemplo en el castigo.

LA GRAN COMEDIA DE GVSTOS, Y DISGVSTOS SON NO MAS QVE IMAGINACION.

DE DON PEDRO CALDERON.

PERSONAS.

El Rey Don Pedro.
El Conde Monforte.
Doña Violante dama.
Eluira dama.
La Reyna D. Maria.
Leonor dueña.
Don Guillen.
Don Vicente.
Chocolate gracioso.

IORNADA PRIMERA.

Salen por vna puerta el Conde, y Violante su hija, y acompañamiento; y por otra Doña Eluira.

Elu. Tened, no passeis de aqui,
señor Conde, porque en esta
florida estacion, que el Mayo
fabricò a la primauera.

VERDADERA QUINTA PARTE DE COMEDIAS

DE

DON PEDRO CALDERON DE LA BARCA,

CAVALLERO DEL ORDEN DE SANTIAGO,
Capellan de Honor de ſu Mageſtad, y de los
ſeñores Reyes Nuevos de la Santa Igleſia
de la Ciudad de Toledo, cèlebre
Poeta Eſpañol.

QUE PUBLICA.

DON JUAN DE VERA TASSIS
y Villarroel Choroniſta de ſu Mageſtad en eſtos
Reynos de Caſtilla, y Leon, y Fiſcal de las
Comedias de Eſpaña.

CON PRIVILEGIO:

EN MADRID: Por *Franciſco Sanz*, Impreſſor del Reyno, y Portero
de Camara de ſu Mageſtad, Año de 1621.

In edition P the play, in quarto form, consists of 47 pages which occupy folios 66v-89v and signatures J (2)-M (each of eight folios). Consecutive foliation appears in the upper right-hand corner of each *recto*. At the bottom of each page is found the first word of the first verse corresponding to the following page.

The text of P displays characteristics that are typical of seventeenth-century typography: [7] The long gothic *s* is used within words either in single or double form but without consistency. It is also used initially, except when the word requires a capital letter. In some instances, again without consistency, the gothic *s* is followed by a roman *s*. A grave accent is used throughout the text, however, words currently accented do not always bear the accent *(aqui, obligacion, melancolia)*. Punctuation is extremely irregular. Periods or question marks usually end a sentence, but other punctuation is arbitrarily, though not entirely, omitted. Commas and colons are superfluously inserted. When space can not accommodate the verse, *n* is replaced by a tilde *(cãsais, biẽ, quiẽ)*; *que* is abbreviated *q̃*, and *aunque* becomes *aunq̃* under similar circumstances.

Orthography throughout the work is not always consistent. Initial *b* and *v* alternate, though rarely *(buelta, bolviendo)*. *J* and *I* alternate at times: as in *Jaime*. The exclamation «Ah!» is found as «Ha!» *U* replaces *b* and *v* *(lleua, siruen)*. The *h*, especially when used with forms of the verb *haber* is arbitrary *(auia, has, ay)*. In some instances *y* arbitrarily replaces *i* *(desayres, Reyna, trayciones)*. *V* always replaces *u* in the indefinite articles: *vn, vna, vno*. In the verb *dejar* the *x* invariably replaces

---

[7] Emilio COTARELO Y MORI, *Fonología española: pronunciación de los siglos XVI y XVII* (Madrid: Imprenta de la Revista de Archivos, 1909).

j (dexar), but in other words the change is not always consistent; it is evident in words such as *xabali, baxeza.* In the verb *hacer* the *z* replaces *c (hazer),* while in some words the *ç* occurs replacing the *z (braços, fuerças).* At times the *z* alternates with *c* in *ce* combinations *(zeloso, pazes, vozes); vencer,* however, is spelled in the modern manner. The *ll* at times replaces the infinitive *-ar* ending plus pronoun *(alvergalle* for *alvergarle).* Some words containing the *cu* combination appear as *qu (quanto, quando, quarto, quatro). Ahora* appears either as *aora* or *agora.* The contraction *del* appears with an accent *(dél)* with the preposition followed by the subject pronoun *él.* Nouns deemed to be important in context are capitalized *(Magestad, Don, Doña, Rey, Reyna, Damas* and even words such as *Cielo* and *Estrella).* The usual words with spelling peculiar to the sixteenth and seventeenth centuries appear throughout *(mesmo* alternating with *mismo; desta, aquesta* alternating with *esta);* words with the consonant clusters *ct* and *pt* appear without the *c* or *p (efeto, conceto);* and *victoria* at times appears as *vitoria.*

Though the type of P is clear and legible, the layout is not always attractive and pleasant. On occasion the columns are spaced too close together, causing some difficulty in distinguishing where one column ends and the other begins. The title of the play and the name of Calderón, appearing always at the top of each folio, are placed too close to the top of the page; the resulting effect of these conditions is that the page always looks more cluttered than it otherwise would be. There are some passages that indicate that the printer was not entirely sure of what he was printing since the sense of the verse is not clear. Changes appearing in subsequent editions, primarily the *Verdadera quinta parte,* correct errors which obscure the meaning of verses in P. For example, in the first scene, a line indispensable for the *romance* rhyme scheme (e-a), is completely omitted in the *princeps* edition. This results in breaking the metric form used in that passage. It occurs after Violante says to the Queen: «Quien humilde / a tus pies, tus manos besa» (verses 65-66). A line was needed to fall between the e-a rhyme of that line and the one following, uttered by the Queen: «Violante, estés norabuena» (verse 68). It must be assumed that Vera Tassis effected the needed change either from copies belonging to actors or producers or by arbitrarily inserting a verse of his own making as he was wont to do.

Other omissions give evidence of negligence in proofreading. This condition is clearly noticeable in the scene in which Chocolate is apprehended by the King and Don Guillén. In the *princeps* edition Chocolate humorously answers his pursuers when ordered to halt:

> Más dificultoso fuera
> el decirme que anduviese,
> cuando, al tener ocho piernas,
> me hubiera quebrado nueve.
> (verses 2367-2370)

Confusion arises, however, when the next two lines read: «Siempre que a escoger me dan, / lo mejor escojo siempre» (verses 2373-2374). The lack of unity between these two thoughts makes the omission of important lines obvious. Again, the Vera Tassis edition fills in the verses which are needed to give logic to Chocolate's retort. The insertion of the King's admonishment: «Dime quién eres, o aquí / hoy a morir te resuelve» (verses 2371-2372) makes Chocolate's response coherent and meaningful. Items listed in the «Variants» part of this study point out similar omissions.

VT, also in quarto form, consists of 41 pages. On the top right-hand corner of the first page the marking «Num. 208» is printed in bold type. Consecutive foliation appears in the upper right-hand corner of each *recto* (1-21). (The play begins and ends on unnumbered pages). It includes signatures A-E_4 (each of four folios) plus the first half of the following folio — signature F. As in P, at the bottom of each page is found the first word of the first verse corresponding to the following page. With few exceptions, the same spelling and printing peculiarities evident in P are to be discerned in VT. Some changes, however, do occur: *jabali* appears in modern spelling; *u* no longer replaces *b* and *v,* although they continue to alternate as in P; *alvergarle* replaces *alvergalle; Miravalle* replaces *Miraballe.* There is some alteration in punctuation which in some instances helps to clarify the meaning of passages. The type of VT is reasonably sharp and clear and can be read with no difficulty, although the print is considerably smaller. Due to the smaller type used in this edition, the play has six pages fewer than P. Aesthetically, VT is more pleasing to the eye since the layout provides for more ample margins. Regretably, as in P, too narrow a space was allowed on the top of the page, resulting in an unwarranted amount of crowding on the vertical.

While *Gustos y disgustos* has been included in the *Partes* and the *Escogidas* already mentioned, the play has also appeared in other collections. Various *sueltas* of the play have also been known to make their way into private collections and into collections of college and university libraries. A list of editions of *Gustos y disgustos* follows, beginning with the seventeenth century and ending with the twentieth:

Gustos y disgustos son no más que imaginación in *Comedias nuevas escogidas de los mejores ingenios de España.* Octava parte. Madrid: Andrés García de la Iglesia, 1657.

Gustos y disgustos son no más que imaginación in *Verdadera quinta parte de comedias de don Pedro Calderón de la Barca ... que publica don Juan de Vera Tassis y Villarroel.* Madrid: Francisco Sanz, 1682.

Gustos y disgustos son no más que imaginación in *Verdadera quinta parte de comedias de don Pedro Calderón de la Barca ... que publica don Juan de Vera Tassis y Villarroel.* Madrid: Francisco Sanz, 1694.

Gustos y disgustos son no más que imaginación in *Verdadera quinta parte de comedias de don Pedro Calderón de la Barca ... que publica don Juan de Vera Tassis y Villarroel.* Madrid: Herederos de Juan García Infanzón, 1730.

Gustos y disgustos son no más que imaginación. Madrid: Antonio Sanz, 1748.

Gustos y disgustos son no más que imaginación in *Comedias del célebre poeta español don Pedro Calderón de la Barca ... que saca a luz don Juan Fernández de Aponte.* Madrid: Viuda de don Manuel Fernández, 1760-63. Vol. X.

Gustos y disgustos son no más que imaginación. Barcelona: Carlos Sapera, 1765.

There are several *sueltas* which appear with either no date or are simply listed as pertaining to the eighteenth century. The title is given exactly as it appears in the catalogues and bibliographies:

La gran comedia. Gustos y disgustos, son, no más que imaginación ... Fiesta que se representó a sus Magestades en el salón de su Real Palacio. (Pp. 1-48 of the Wayne State University—Apontes Collection, Vol. VI, No. CV 21.)[8] N.p., n.d.

Gustos y disgustos son no más que imaginación. Barcelona: Francisco Suria y Burgada, n.d.

---

[8] B. B. Ashcom, *A Descriptive Catalogue of the Spanish Comedias Sueltas in the Wayne State University Library and the Private Library of Professor B. B. Ashcom* (Detroit: Wayne State University Libraries, 1965), p. 40.

La Gran Comedia, Gustos y disgustos son, no más que imaginación ... Fiesta que se representó a sus Magestades en el Salón de su Real Palacio. (Wayne State University No. 208.)[9] N.p., n.d.

Comedia famosa. Gustos y disgustos son no más que imaginación. N.p., n.d.

Gustos y disgustos son no más que imaginación. Comedia famosa. Sevilla: Diego López de Haro, n.d.

Gustos y disgustos son no más que imaginación in *Teatro español o colección de dramas escogidos.* Londres: E. Justins, 1820. Tomo II.

Gustos y disgustos son no más que imaginación in *Las comedias de D. Pedro Calderón de la Barca, cotejadas con las mejores ediciones hasta ahora publicadas, corregidas y dadas a luz por Juan Jorge Keil.* Leipsique, 1827-30.

Gustos y disgustos son no más que imaginación in *Biblioteca de autores españoles. Colección hecha ... por D. Juan Eugenio Hartzenbusch.* Madrid, 1848. Vol. IV.

Gustos y disgustos son no más que imaginación. Barcelona, 1886.

Gustos y disgustos son no más que imaginación in *Don Pedro Calderón de la Barca. Obras completas. Edición, prólogo y notas por el prof. Ángel Valbuena Briones.* Madrid: Aguilar, 1960. Vol. II.

Judging by the number of *sueltas* appearing in the eighteenth century, *Gustos y disgustos* was not entirely lacking in appeal to the reading public. Gradually the play seems to have lost popularity. In the twentieth century only one edition has been published. The end result is that the play has fallen into relative obscurity, and very few Spanish students know of its existence.

An investigation of documents pertaining to the record of performances of the play leaves one with the impres-

[9] I believe this *suelta* derives from the *Verdadera quinta parte* of 1694. The description in the Wayne State University Library catalogue and the No. 208 preceding the title of the *comedia* coincide with a copy of the *Verdadera quinta parte* which I obtained from the Biblioteca Nacional of Madrid.

sion that although the play was never completely abandoned, it was, nevertheless, not a favorite of acting companies. The play is known to have been performed in Madrid, Valencia, and Valladolid; there is no record of performances in Seville. In his book on the life and works of Calderón, Emilio Cotarelo y Mori [10] makes mention of a trip to Valencia which Calderón took in 1638. The passage refers to the *fiestas centenarias* (celebrating the anniversary of the conquest of Valencia) in connection with a presentation of *Gustos y disgustos:*

> Habíase tratado antes desto de que alguno de los valencianos ingenios se dispusiera a escribir una comedia de la historia de la conquista de Valencia, por ser a propósito para la fiesta y haber en Valencia muchos sujetos que la podrían disponer muy ingeniosa y entretenida. Pero no fué posible que esto tuviera efecto por haberse acordado tarde; y aunque la brevedad del tiempo no hubiera sido parte para que no se hiciera, pero lo fué para que los representantes no la pudieran estudiar, con que se hubo de elegir la comedia que se intitula *Gustos y disgustos son no más que imaginación,* porque ésta trata parte de la historia del rey don Pedro, que fué padre del rey don Jaime, y es una de las que han ayudado a extender por España la noticia del único ingenio de don Pedro Calderón que pocos meses antes había estado en Valencia y dejado en ella muchos aficionados a la nobleza de su proceder y muchos envidiosos de su milagroso caudal. [11]

From the foregoing, one may deduce that *Gustos y disgustos* was not a new play at the time and that it must have been presented with enough frequency to have made the actors feel sufficiently familiar with the work to be able to perform it without rehearsal. Cotarelo y Mori records, furthermore, that the play was performed

[10] *Ensayo sobre la vida y obras de D. Pedro Calderón de la Barca* (Madrid, 1924), p. 196.

[11] COTARELO Y MORI, *Ensayo,* p. 197.

by a well-known company of players under the direction of Bartolomé Romero. Among the actors were Alonso de Osuna (apparently quite famous in his time), Antonia Manuela Catalán (wife of the director), Robledo (a character actor of good reputation), and Diego de Mencos (a *gracioso).*

The earliest performance for which any official documentation exists took place in Madrid in 1661. In *Memorias de la Real Academia Española,* document number 169 states:

> Certificación del Escribano del Ayuntamiento de que no había representación en el corral de la Cruz, y que en el del Príncipe, la compañía de Escamilla, había puesto carteles para hacer la comedia de *El Gusto y disgusto sólo es imaxinación.* Madrid, 18 de Abril de 1661. (Archivo Municipal, 2ª, 468-29.) [12]

Although the title of the play is only slightly altered in the preceding document, the alteration appears more obvious in another entry from the same source. Document number 173 states:

> Fe de notario de que hoy no ha representado Antonio de Escamilla en el corral del Príncipe «porque la compañía estuvo en la sala del Ayuntamiento de Madrid, representando al Consejo Real de Castilla la comedia de *Dicha y desdicha no es más que imaginación»* Madrid, 13 de Noviembre de 1661. (Archivo Municipal, 2ª, 468-29.) [13]

Narciso Alonso Cortés gives a complete record of the plays performed in Valladolid between April 7, 1681 and February 20, 1798. *Gustos y disgustos,* it is interesting to note, appears only once in a period of over a hundred

---

[12] (Madrid: Hijos de Reus, 1910), X, 29.
[13] (Madrid: Hijos de Reus, 1910), X, 30.

years. The *comedia* was presented December 4, 1691 by «la compañía de Manuel Ángel y Fabiana Laura.» [14]

The record of performances in the eighteenth century is only slightly more impressive than in the seventeenth. In the course of a decade, the play was presented a total of five times in the Teatro Príncipe in Madrid: April 11 and 12, 1785, March 17 and 20, 1787, and October 27, 1794. [15]

During the nineteenth century the play was revived again. Five more performances were given within the space of one year. The *Cartelera madrileña* [16] indicates that the play was performed on June 11, 1830, September 1 and 2, 1830, and June 16 and 17, 1831. After the nineteenth century the record is incomplete. From the scarcity of performances during the periods for which records are available, it is easy to surmise that the play never achieved a high level of popularity.

---

[14] *Teatro en Valladolid* (Madrid: Tip. de la Revista de Archivos, 1923), p. 306.

[15] Ada M. Coe, *Catálogo bibliográfico y crítico de las comedias anunciadas en los periódicos de Madrid* ... (Baltimore: Johns Hopkins Press, 1935), pp. 107-108.

[16] *Cuadernos bibliográficos. Cartelera teatral madrileña,* ed. por el Seminario de bibliografía hispánica de la facultad de filosofía y letras de Madrid (Madrid: Consejo Superior de Investigaciones Científicas, 1961), p. 9.

CHAPTER II

HISTORICAL BACKGROUND

Serving as a point of departure to the plot of *Gustos y disgustos son no más que imaginación* is an incident in medieval Spanish history. Some chroniclers give no credibility to the incident in question, taking it to be mere legend; others accept it as authentic without reservation. Central figures in this occurrence are the King Don Pedro II of Aragon and his Queen Doña María of Montpellier.[1] What is known to be historical fact about the King and his consort is that Don Pedro of Aragon came to the throne in 1196. For reasons of state, he married

[1] The sources of biographical information for this section are:

Antonio Cánovas del Castillo, ed., *Historia general de España* (Madrid: El Progreso, 1893), pp. 195-222.

Modesto Lafuente, *et al.*, *Historia general de España desde los tiempos antiguos hasta la muerte de Fernando VII* (Barcelona: Montaner y Simón, 1888), pp. 352-354.

Doña María of Montpellier in 1204, the same year of his coronation in Rome. Doña María had been previously married to the Count of Cominges and from him she had begotten two sons. It is important to keep this previous marriage in mind, for later Don Pedro will rely on this point in his struggle to divorce his wife.

Even though Doña María, according to some historians, was greatly admired for her many qualities and singular virtues and was also one of the most excellent princesses of her time, she, nevertheless, was never successful in capturing her husband's affection. Shortly after their marriage, Don Pedro tired of his conjugal life with the Queen and left her, distracting himself, not circumspectly, with other ladies of Montpellier where Doña María, herself, lived. The King's extramarital activities resulted in disturbing not only the Queen but also the consuls and grandees of Montpellier who looked upon the monarch's conduct with disfavor and disapproval. Tormented by the fact that the royal estrangement would result in the lack of successor to the Queen who was also their Countess, the advisors and grandees were at the same time very critical of the lack of decorum displayed by Don Pedro toward this woman whose honor they guarded jealously.

Wishing to put an end to this marriage of convenience that had resulted only in making him unhappy, Don Pedro went to Rome to plead his case with the Pontiff. While the King's request for divorce was still under deliberation by Pope Innocent III and other religious authorities, the year 1207 rolled around, and with it came the birth of his son, the famous Don Jaime *el Conquistador*.

The birth of the prince, however, did not suffice to deter the King Don Pedro in his efforts to have his marriage to Doña María declared null. The legal battle continued for a long time, lasting until 1213, the year in which the Queen herself went to Rome and obtained a favorable verdict from the Pontiff. The King obstinately refused to accede to the conjugal union, and as a consequence Pope Innocent III advised the bishops of Avignon and Carcasson to compel the monarch to abide by the pontifical decision by threat of ecclesiastical censure with no right of appeal. The King, nevertheless, persevered in his enterprise, and the Queen remained in Rome to await the Pope's ultimate judgment. Meanwhile, the King Don Pedro passed on and his demise at last put an end to the scandalous maneuverings that threatened to jeopardize the Christian faith.

More prodigious are the circumstances which transpired in the conception and birth of Don Jaime. The event, written by the monarch himself, appears in the *Crónica* or *Comentarios* of his life. His account, in which he employes the royal «we», is literally translated into English from the transcription made by Menéndez y Pelayo. [2]

> Now we shall relate in what manner we were begotten and in what manner our birth came about. Our father, the King Don Pedro, did not want to see our mother, the Queen, and it happened that one day the King, our Father, was in Lates, and the Queen, our mother, was in Miravals. And a grandee who went by the name of Guillén de Alcalá came to my father, and so entreated him that he made him come to Miravals, where the Queen our mother was staying. And that night that both spent in Miravals, Our Lord willed that we be begotten. And when the Queen our mother felt herself to be impregnated, she went to Montpellier. And our Lord willed that our birth take place there in the house of Tornamira on the eve of Our Lady

[2] Félix Lope de Vega Carpio, *Obras de Lope de Vega,* ed. Marcelino Menéndez y Pelayo (Madrid: Sucesores de Rivadeneyra, 1898), VIII, cxxx-cxxxi.

> of the Candelaria. And after being born, our mother sent us to Santa María, and we were taken in arms. And they were praying the matins in the church of Our Lady, and having made us enter the portico, they sang *Te Deum laudamus*. And the clerics were not aware of our presence there, but we happened to enter when they were singing that cantical. And later we were taken to San Fermín, and at that moment when those who were carrying us entered the church of San Fermín, the *Benedictus Dominus Israel* was being sung. And when they returned us to the house of our mother, she rejoiced much for those prognostications. And she had twelve candles made, all of the same weight and size, and she had them all lighted simultaneously, and gave each one the name of an Apostle, and she promised our Lord that we would be named after the apostle whose candle lasted the longest. And the one of Saint James lasted about three fingers more than the others. And for that reason, and for the grace of God, we were named James. And thus we came from the Queen, who was our mother, and from the King Don Pedro, our father. ... And it seems to be an act of God.

Despite the apocrifal character of Don Jaime's narration, Ramón Muntaner in his chronicle takes the monarch's account to be true without question and adds other ingredients of an even more fabulous nature. Devoting no less than four chapters to the incident, his version acquires a novelistic flavor that surpasses the first one. Muntaner, it is plain to see, was convinced that the birth of Don Jaime was certainly a miraculous act of God. Since it later came to be a principal source of Calderón's play, a summary of Muntaner's account, translated with the aid of Menéndez y Pelayo's transcription, is worthwhile mentioning at this point: [3]

It is a known fact that the King Don Pedro married Doña María of Montpellier, not only because of her noble lineage and good qualities, but also because with the

[3] *Obras*, pp. cxxxii-cxxxvi.

acquisition of Montpellier, he would increase his estate and barony. For a long time after the marriage, the King, who was young and fell in love easily with the genteel ladies, did not live with the Queen. The fact that he would not even go near her when he sometimes went to Montpellier made her vassals, especially her advisors, very unhappy. It became common knowledge that Don Pedro was particularly fond of a certain lady in Montpellier. Knowing of this, the consuls and advisors sought to induce the King's chamberlain and confidant to help them in a conspiracy, promising to make him forever wealthy. They confided in the King's aide the concern that they felt, i.e., the fact that despite the many favorable attributes of Doña María, the King had absented himself from her bed. This deed, in their estimation, was wrong in itself and also the biggest dishonor to the Queen and to Montpellier. If the Queen were not to have a successor, they feared that Montpellier would eventually pass from the kingdom of Aragon to other hands. Assured that the King's chamberlain was willing to help them in their scheme, the advisors disclosed their plan. Realizing that the King's confidant was aware of the monarch's involvement with a certain lady and that the gentleman's duty was to arrange a secret rendezvous between her and Don Pedro, the consuls proposed that the King's aide serve as their mediator. They advised him to tell Don Pedro that he had arranged a meeting with the lady in the King's chambers, but that she requested that there be no light so as not to be seen by anyone. Once the lovers were together, the whole court having retired for the night, all the members of the conspiracy would gather in the Consulate of Montpellier. Among those present would be the twelve consuls, several other important gentlemen and citizens, the Queen Doña María with twelve very honorable *dueñas* and twelve maidens, two public notaries, the

Bishop's official, two canons, and four good clerics. Each man and woman was to carry a candle that was to be lighted when the Queen entered the King's chambers in lieu of his paramour. All would remain at the door until daybreak when the King's chamberlain was to open the door. Once the door was opened, everybody with lighted tapers in hand was to enter the King's quarters. The scheme would then be disclosed to Don Pedro.

The King's aide agreed to act as mediator but asked that other details be added to the plan. He advised that in honor of God and Our Lady of Valluert (being that on that day, Saturday, they had begun to discuss this matter) during the whole seven days following, beginning on Monday, every presbiter and ordained priest sing masses to Our Lady in honor of the seven joys which she had for her Son. He hoped that this act of devotion would please her so that God would give them pleasure and happiness in their efforts, and that from this endeavor would come the fruit through which the kingdom of Aragon, the counties of Barcelona, Urgel and Montpellier, and the rest of the land might be provided with a good lord. He further proposed that the eve of the following Sunday they also have masses sung in Santa María *de les Taules* and in Santa María de Valluert. All agreed to this, and they also ordered that on that Sunday all the citizens of Montpellier should be in the churches keeping vigil and praying while the Queen would be with the King. As a final measure of holy devotion to their endeavor, it was ordained that everybody should fast on bread and water on Saturday.

All together, the members of the Council went to the Queen Doña María and told her of the plan which they had devised. The Queen was very thankful for their prudence and agreed to take part in the stratagem. The mediator, according to plan, arranged the rendezvous. Sunday night, while everyone in the palace slept, the previously mentioned personages, each with a lighted candle in hand, entered the palace and arrived en masse at the door of the King's chambers. At this point the Queen entered the room while the entourage remained outside praying. The royal couple remained in solace, the King believing all along that he had his mistress by his side and not his wife. That night all the churches of Montpellier remained open, and the whole town was to be found in them, praying as planned. At dawn the notables, prelates, clerics and ladies, each with his lighted taper entered the monarch's room. The startled King who lay with his wife, jumped out of bed, drawing his sword. All who were present knelt, bidding their King to see who the person was that lay sleeping by his side. The Queen then arose, and the King recognized her. The well-intentioned conspiracy was confided to the King. Don Pedro answered that as long as they had planned the deed in that manner, he prayed to God that their purpose would be accomplished.

That day, however, the King Don Pedro left Montpellier. The Queen's advisors gathered six of the gentlemen whom the monarch held in highest regard, and along with all those involved in bringing the royal couple together (including the two notaries who in the presence of the King had made note of what had transpired) ordered them not to leave the palace but to remain by the Queen's side until nine months had passed. The King's chamberlain was also to remain in the company of the Queen. All were exceedingly joyful upon seeing that their efforts had produced good results, for the Queen did in fact conceive and at the end of nine months gave birth to a child who in time was to become famous for the deeds performed for the betterment of his people and for championing the Christian faith. With great rejoicing the infant was baptized in the church of Nuestra Señora Sta. María *de les Taules* of Montpellier, receiving the name of Jaime.

Falling between the accounts of Don Jaime and that of Muntaner is the one offered by Bernardo Desclot. His version is less novelistic than Muntaner's, but offers more details than Don Jaime. Differing from the two mentioned ones in various aspects, he attributes the subterfuge to the Queen Doña María with the aid of her majordomo. He does not make mention of the name of Don Guillén de Alcalá as the go-between. Omitting all the data pertinent to the intervention of the consuls, barons, and grandees of Montpellier, his version lends verisimilitude to the incident.

From a study of these Catalan chronicles it can be surmised in what manner the legend grew, originating in the simple narration of Don Jaime, gradually gaining embellishment in succeeding accounts. Stripped of all extraneous, apocrifal trappings, the anecdote of the unusual circumstances of the begetting of Don Jaime el Conquistador remains. The monarch attests not only to this, but also to the important role attributed to the mediator, Don Guillén de Alcalá. The name of Alcalá has continued to appear in succeeding chronicles and histories, among which are the *Anales de la Corona de Aragón* by Gerónimo de Zurita.[4] His account bears a remarkable resemblance to the one originally offered by Don Jaime.

In *Silva de varia lección,* a book of miscellany which appeared in 1556, the incident of the stratagem is also recorded. Heading the chapter is this resumé which appears in capital letters:

[4] (Zaragoza: Diego Dormer, 1469), I, fol. 96.

DE UN MUY HERMOSO ENGAÑO QUE UNA REINA DE ARAGÓN HIZO AL REY, SU MARIDO; Y CÓMO FUÉ ENGENDRADO EL REY DON JAIME DE ARAGÓN, SU HIJO; Y DE SU NACIMIENTO Y MUERTE.[5]

Pero Mejía, the author of this book of random information, recalls having read the incident in the histories of the Kings of Aragon. With minor variations, his rendition follows the ones previously cited. Mejía, like Desclot, attributes the plot to Doña María, but with the help of the King's chamberlain. No mention of the grandees and dignitaries of the court is made by this author either. This version varies also in that the King, believing that the Queen is his mistress, seeks to guard her secret. At dawn he tells her to leave so that she will avoid being discovered. At that point the Queen decides to drop the masquerade saying to him:

> Señor y marido mío: no soy yo la que pensáis: sabed que con vuestra mujer habéis estado esta noche; vos hacéme el mal que quisierdes, que yo no me iré de aquí hasta que algunas personas dignas de fe me vean con vos en la cama, porque si Dios me hubiere hecho la merced que le he pedido, de que yo de vos concibiese, quiero que haya testigos de haberme visto con vos.[6]

The King takes the deception as prudent and honest. Bearing no malice toward his wife's astuteness, he summons two honorable gentlemen to be witness to the Queen's integrity.

---

[5] *Silva de varia lección* (Madrid: Sociedad de bibliófilos españoles, 1934), II, 135.

[6] *Silva de varia lección,* p. 136.

CHAPTER III

SOURCES OF THE PLAY AND LITERARY DIFFUSION OF THE THEME

Gustos y disgustos son no más que imaginación, an intriguing *comedia palaciega,* is without question based on a popular legend about the King and Queen of Aragon, Don Pedro and Doña María. In the play, mention is made of the portentous birth of their son, Jaime I, later called the Conqueror. The anecdote, as we have seen, had been recorded in the ancient Catalan *crónicas* (Jaime I, Desclot, and Muntaner). It had also appeared in the chronicles of Beurot and Zurita, before passing on to the miscellany, *Silva de varia lección* of Pero Mejía.

Any discussion of the sources of the play, *Gustos y disgustos,* must of necessity be regarded as a matter of conjecture. In all likelihood, Calderón was as familiar with the chronicles that made mention of the incident as he was with Mejía's book. It is also very probable that Calderón was familiar with the works of other writers who had treated the theme. According to Menéndez y Pelayo, Mateo Bandello, among whose novels are many which are historical anecdotes, was the first to employ the incident as a theme in his novel, *Inganno della reina d'Aragona al re Pietro, su marito, per aver da lei figiuoli.* [1] The Italian novelist confesses having heard the story from a Spanish gentleman, Ramiro Torrilla, who in Menéndez y Pelayo's judgment must have been acquainted with the chronicles of Don Jaime and Desclot, but not with Muntaner's. This opinion is borne out by the fact that Bandello attributes the astuteness of the trick played on the King, not to the nobles of Montpellier, but to the Queen. Furthermore, Bandello incorporated the prognostications of the *Te Deum laudamus* and the *Benedictus* and the vignette of the twelve tapers. Bandello, in keeping with the style of the Italian novellas, gives the story a ribald treatment. Contrary to historical fact, in the Italian version, the King ultimately falls in love with the Queen.

The *romance* found in the *Rosa gentil* by Timoneda seems to have borrowed elements from diverse sources. The narrative is reminiscent of Muntaner's in the religious aspect, yet suggests influence from Bandello or Pero Mejía in its inclusion of the two gentlemen who are summoned to attest to the Queen's honor after having spent the night in the King's chambers:

[1] Félix Lope de Vega Carpio, *Obras de Lope de Vega,* ed. Marcelino Menéndez y Pelayo (Madrid: Sucesores de Rivadeneyra, 1898), VIII, cxli.

Romance del nascimiento
del Rey don Jayme[2]

Angustiada esta la Reyna,
y no sin mucha razon
porque su marido el Rey,
don Pedro Rey de Aragon
no hazia caso della
mas que si fuera varon
ni le pagaua la deuda
que tenia obligacion,
antes con otras mugeres
era su delectacion.
Lo que mas la fatigaua,
y le daua mas passion,
no era por el deleyte
de la tal conuersacion,
si no que de su marido
no tenia generacion
para gouernar el Reyno
sin ninguna diuision,
porque muerto el rey se espera
en su Reyno confusion.
Contempla la noble Reyna
la rebulta y turbacion
que podia padescer
Cataluña, y Aragon:
bueltos los ojos al Cielo
con muy grande deuocion
supplicaua a Jesu Christo
por su sagrada passion
que a su señor y marido
le pusiesse en coraçon
que se juntasse con ella
con sana, y limpia intencion.
No dexaua monesterios,
ni casa de religion,
que no mandasse hazer
cada dia oracion.

---

[2] Juan TIMONEDA, *Rosas de romances* (Valencia: Editorial Castalia, 1936), pp. lx-lxii.

Estando la noble Reyna
con esta sancta oppinion,
vino le al pensamiento
vna loable inuencion,
y es, que supo por muy cierto,
y por vera relacion,
que el Rey era namorado,
y amaua de coraçon
vna dama muy hermosa
de gentil dispusicion.
Hablo con el Camarero
sin aguardar mas sazon
que al Rey solia seruir
en esta negociacion.
Si me tienes muy secreta
de mi hauras buen gualardon.
Tu has de dar a entender
al rey con gran discrecion,
que essa dama a quien el sirue
verna sin mas dilacion
a dormir con su Alteza,
mas con esta condicion
que en su pieça no aya lumbre,
para mas reputacion.
Concertada con el rey
aquesta visitacion,
la reyna vino a la noche
y tuuo recreacion
con el rey a su plazer
con gran dissimulacion.
El rey quando vio que el dia
venia sin detencion,
por complir con su palabra
que otorgo a la exclamacion
dixo, Señora leuanta,
vete en paz pues ay sason.
La reyna entonces le dizo:
no soy la que pensays non:
sabed que con vuestra muger
tuuistes conuersacion:
vos hazedme bien o mal,
quiera que aya de esto en hombres

de fee, como en vnion
nos han visto a los dos juntos
y de esto hos pido perdon.
El rey tomo aquel engaño
como cuerdo y buen varon:
llamo dos hombres de salua
por dar cabo a su oppinion.
En fin que la reyna hizo
entonces buena oracion,
que de la burla, preñada
quedo de vn lindo garçon.
El qual nascido don Jayme
le llama, y dio bendicion.
Este fue rey tan nombrado
rey don Jayme de Aragon:
este gano a Valencia,
Mallorca, y su poblacion.

Lope de Vega, who must have been well acquainted with all of the sources cited above, is the author of *La reina doña María,* a play in which he employs the same theme. (Menéndez y Pelayo believes the play was written after 1618.) Intentionally rearranging names and deeds, Lope conveniently mixed historical fact with fable to suit his own design: Don Pedro's coronation in Rome takes place in the same scene in which he pleads with the Pontiff for a divorce from Doña María. Don Guillén de Alcalá, portrayed as brother of the Queen, is dispossessed of lands in Montpellier.

Lope's unique contribution to the diffusion of the theme rests on his having attributed the deception of the King, not to the perspicacity of the Queen Doña María (as did Desclot, Bandello, and Mejía), nor to the citizens of Montpellier (as did Muntaner), but to the King's paramour, Doña Juana. The latter in this case does not love the monarch, and she feels great compassion for Doña María, the disdained wife. In his version Lope avoids the actual bedroom scene of the rendezvous, allowing a minor character to allude to the event some time after the birth of Don Jaime.

Guillén de Castro undertook a treatment of the theme in *El perfecto caballero.* The play first appeared in published form in the *Primera Parte* of his *Obras* (1621). It was later reproduced in the collection *Comedias de los mejores y más insignes ingenios de España,* published in Lisbon in 1652.[3] In recent years another edition has been published by Eduardo Juliá Martínez.

In this work, the anecdote is employed in a different manner. Not only is the locale changed, but also the ending: the King is murdered. The plot revolves around an Italian King and Queen from Naples. The Italian monarch, like the Spanish Don Pedro, loathes his wife and loves Diana, sister of Ludovico. The latter is in love with the Queen, even though the King has been led to believe that he is her brother. Don Jaime Centellas, father of Miguel *(el perfecto caballero),* seeing the wretched state of the Queen, suggests to her the employment of the subterfuge which Doña María of Montpellier had used with her husband. The Queen takes the advice, involving Diana in her plot. The event turns to tragedy when Ludovico, who is in love with the Queen, takes the place of the King in the Queen's chambers. In the end Diana is saved from dishonor, the King dies by the hand of Ludovico who wins the favor of the Queen and her subjects by denouncing the dead monarch as a tyrannical ruler.

---

[3] GUILLÉN DE CASTRO, *Obras de D. Guillén de Castro y Bellvis,* ed. Eduardo Juliá Martínez (Madrid: Tip. de la Revista de Archivos, 1926), II, ix.

CHAPTER IV

ANALYSIS OF THE PLAY

Synopsis of the Play

ACT I

Count Monforte and Violante, his daughter, are paying a visit to the Queen, Doña María, at the royal country villa in Miravalle. Accompanied by Elvira, the Queen's lady in waiting, Violante goes to pay her respects to the Queen, who is sleeping in the garden. Upon awakening, Doña María relates her dream to Violante and Elvira. She tells them of the brief happiness which she experienced, dreaming of giving birth to a son, Don Jaime el Conquistador.

Don Pedro is carried unconscious into the Queen's chambers by his attendants, Don Guillén and Don Vicente de Fox. Chocolate, the *gracioso* and lackey to Don Vicente, explains that the King has fallen from a runaway horse while chasing a wild boar in the nearby hunting grounds of the villa. Although entreated by the Queen to remain in the villa and be cared for, Don Pedro obstinately refuses to stay, claiming to have business at court. The King's amorous attentions to Violante are as evident as his loathing for the Queen. Furthermore, Don Vicente is annoyed, for he himself and Violante are secretly in love.

Later in Zaragoza, the Conde in conversation with his daughter alludes to the bad blood that exists between Monforte and the House of Fox. Count Monforte expresses strong disapproval of the attention paid Violante by Don Vicente whom he considers his enemy and forbids her to see him further. That evening, Leonor, servant to Violante, having been bribed by the King's confidant, Don Guillén, makes preparations for a night visit from the King by leaving the balcony door open and by throwing a rope to facilitate his entrance. Accompanied by Chocolate, Don Vicente arrives first. He confesses to Violante his jealousy of the King's amorous behavior at court. In the midst of her conversation her father calls to Violante and she leaves abruptly; Don Vicente and Chocolate are left in total darkness. As Don Pedro enters through the balcony, Don Vicente and Chocolate take cover. Violante returns to discover the presence of the unexpected caller, the King. As the latter is declaring his love to Violante, Don Vicente emerges from the shadowy darkness. He confides that Violante and he are secretly betrothed and warns Don Pedro not to dishonor him through his illicit love for Violante.

Hearing the murmur of conversation, Count Monforte arrives on the scene. At the approaching footsteps of the Conde, the King and Don Vicente quickly mask themselves with their cloaks. Count Monforte demands an explanation from his daughter for the presence of the two men in the house at this late hour of the night. Violante replies that the King will give an explanation and she leaves. The King, side-stepping the dilemma, says that Don Vicente will give the explanation and the monarch also takes leave. At first, Count Monforte surmises that Don Pedro has come to the house as an intermediary for Don Vicente to ask for Violante's hand in marriage. Don Vicente confesses that Violante and he have been secretly in love for two years. Furthermore, he adds that both his honor and that of the Conde are in peril because of the King's daring nighttime entry into the house. Don Vicente asks to marry Violante and Count Monforte regrets permitting his daughter to marry an arch enemy. Realizing that he would regret even more the loss of his honor, the Conde promises to give his answer to Don Vicente the following day in the King's chambers.

ACT II

At court the following day Count Monforte requests the King's permission to marry his daughter to Don Vicente; Don Pedro grants it. Returning home, the Conde asks Don Vicente to wait outside while he gives Violante the happy news. Hearing her father's sanction of her marriage, Violante believes his declaration merely to be a ruse designed to make her confess her guilt for associating with the very man to whom her father once forbade her to speak. Seeking to save the situation and in an effort to prevent possible chastisement by her father, Violante employs trickery in replying that she would never marry Don Vicente even if the penalty were death.

The reply is shocking to Count Monforte and makes him wonder if Don Vicente has tricked him into consenting to the marriage. Don Vicente who is eavesdropping the conversation is also stunned by the reply. Nevertheless, the Conde feels compelled to proceed with his intentions since the King already has given permission. Count Monforte then orders Don Vicente to enter. Each one doubting the real feelings of the other, all three are in a confused state of mind. Later, however, when left alone, Violante explains to Don Vicente the reason for her strange reply and the lovers rejoice at the resolution of their problem.[1]

At this moment Don Guillén arrives with two letters from the King: one addressed to Violante; the other to Don Vicente. In the letter to Violante the King awards her the *Villa de Castellón* as part of her dowry and bestows upon her the title of *marquesa.* In the letter to Don Vicente the King confers upon him the title of *maestre de campo* and orders him to leave immediately on a campaign to Mallorca. He is placed in command of an army and instructed not to return until the campaign is finished, an obvious move by Don Pedro to get Don Vicente out of the way in order to continue his courtship of Violante.

Violante asks Don Vicente that she be permitted to remain with the Queen during his absence. Her husband agrees but requests that Violante give as the reason for wanting to stay with the Queen Doña María that she wishes to absent herself from her father who harbors an

[1] Although the actual marriage ceremony does not take place on stage, it must be assumed that Don Vicente and Violante are hereafter husband and wife. Throughout the remainder of this synopsis of the play, the terms «husband» and «wife» will be used to designate Don Vicente and Violante, respectively.

ill feeling for having been forced to marry her to his enemy.

At the royal country villa in Miravalle Violante informs the Queen of her marriage and of her impressive dowry. At Violante's request Doña María asks Count Monforte to allow his daughter to remain at the villa. The Conde agrees, but wonders if the Queen's reasons for wanting Violante by her side are based not on affection but rather on jealousy aroused by the King's attentions to Violante.

Later that evening the King, accompanied by Don Guillén, comes to the gardens of the villa in search of Violante. Meanwhile Violante received word from her husband that he will visit her secretly before his departure to Mallorca, and as the King approaches the balcony Violante peers through the window in the garden wall in search of her husband. Incognito, Don Pedro speaks to her but before she is able to identify the voice, he is forced to leave the balcony abruptly as he hears approaching noises; it is Don Vicente and Chocolate. Violante realizes that it was the King to whom she spoke. Fearing to be discovered, she leaves the window. At this moment Don Vicente and Chocolate arrive at the balcony, but finding no one at the window, they leave immediately. In the dark the King mistakes the Queen for Violante. He addresses her as Violante and declares his love. The Queen realizes his mistake but, wishing to find out more, she goes along with the masquerade. In her replies, Doña María expresses her true feelings for her husband without disclosing her true identity. Asked by the King to be allowed to continue the courtship, the Queen accedes to his wishes.

As Don Vicente is approaching for the second time, the Queen leaves the window. Mistaking the shrouded figure of Don Vicente for Don Guillén in the dark, the

King exclaims to him that Violante has allowed him to return the following day. Suddenly realizing that the man to whom he is speaking is not Don Guillén, Don Pedro attempts to uncover the cloaked face of Don Vicente. The latter employs the only means of defense which he has against the King—flight. Don Vicente goes off to war suspecting that he is being dishonored by his wife's infidelity.

ACT III

Accompanied by Don Guillén, the King returns to the window with intentions of speaking to Violante. The Queen continues masquerading as Violante and appears at the window. Don Pedro gives her recent news of her husband: having arranged a peace treaty with the Moors shortly after his arrival in Mallorca, he intends to return sooner than originally anticipated. The King expresses his hopes to continue seeing Violante regularly after her husband's return.

Realizing that the end of her masquerade is near, Doña María informs Don Pedro that she will deny any meetings that occurred during Don Vicente's absence. Startled by a noise of someone approaching, the Queen abruptly leaves the window while the King goes to find out the cause. He sees that Don Guillén has seized one of the intruders—Chocolate. The frightened lackey discloses his identity and informs the King of Don Vicente's return from Mallorca. It is clear to Don Pedro after a few questions now that the mysterious man who took flight from the grounds of the villa recently was Don Vicente. Wishing to warn Violante of her husband's arrival, the King plans to enter Violante's chambers secretly.

Finding his startled lackey, Don Vicente inquires if Chocolate divulged their presence at the villa. Fearing punishment, the *gracioso* replies that he has disclosed nothing. Remembering that he had seen the two men speaking to a woman whom he believes to be his wife, Don Vicente's imagination leads him to doubt his wife's fidelity now more than ever. Despite the circumstantial evidence which points to her guilt, he makes an effort to remove the doubts that plague him; he will have a *desengaño* by coming face to face with his wife. He sends Chocolate to inform Violante of his arrival and of his intention to see her secretly in her chambers even before paying his respects to the King.

As husband and wife meet, Violante's genuine happy greeting convinces Don Vicente (momentarily at least) that his imagination has played tricks on him and that his wife is indeed faithful. The servant Leonor interrupts their embraces to announce the King's arrival at the villa. Don Vicente sees nothing out of the ordinary in the arrival of Don Pedro at his own royal villa. When Leonor adds that the King is coming directly to Violante's room rather than to the Queen's chambers, Don Vicente's suspicions are aroused anew. Realizing that her fidelity is suspect, Violante feigns calmness as she explains that the King's actions are merely evidence of his customary intent to avoid his wife's presence. Don Vicente questions Violante's lack of surprise, implying in his retort that Don Pedro has no doubt visited her room many times in the past. Violante truthfully answers that she has neither seen nor spoken to the King since her husband's departure. Still vacillating between trust and distrust, Don Vicente attributes his disquiet to fear at being discovered in Violante's room before paying proper respects to the King.

As the King and his confidant enter, Don Vicente and Chocolate take cover. Violante is glad to have her husband within hearing distance so that he may discover for himself that his suspicions are indeed ill-founded. When Don Pedro inquires if Violante has seen Don Vicente, she replies in the negative. The King warns her that Don Vicente is aware of their secret meetings and that her life is in peril. At Violante's denial of having had any meetings with the King, he insists that though Violante vowed to deny their rendezvous, she must take heed of his warning because in keeping with the social code Don Vicente has returned with intentions of killing her to avenge his honor. At this point Don Vicente is unequivocally convinced of his wife's unfaithfulness and resigns himself to kill her and restore his honor.

The Queen arrives to reprimand the King for failing to appear at *her* chambers and not Violante's. Don Pedro claims to have mistaken Violante's room for the Queen's. As Doña María leads the King and Don Guillén away, Don Vicente draws his dagger to kill Violante, but his deed is thwarted as she is summoned by the Queen. Don Vicente decides to return later when Violante will be alone in her room.

Violante realizes now that to return to her room means her death, yet staying away confirms her guilt. If she were convinced that her death would remedy her husband's anxiety, she would gladly die. Her sense of honor, however, compels her to stay her death until Don Vicente has had more opportunity to discover his error.

Count Monforte finds Violante in a confused state of mind. Assuring him of her innocence, Violante confides her dilemma to her father. The Conde is prepared to confront Don Vicente to defend his daughter's life and honor.

Later, at a prearranged signal, the King, in a final amorous endeavor to win Violante's love, goes to the window. Don Vicente also comes to the window intending to kill his wife. The Queen approaches the window ready to reveal her true identity to her husband. Not recognizing each other in the dark, Don Vicente and Don Pedro draw their swords intending to fight. At the sound of clashing swords, Don Guillén and Elvira arrive at the scene with a lantern. Presently, Count Monforte and Violante arrive also. The light cast by the lantern reveals the identities of the three characters at the window. Don Vicente, discovering that he is dueling with the King, begs forgiveness. Don Pedro realizes that the woman at the window is Doña María and not Violante. The Queen confesses her masquerade and is pardoned by the King who accepts her love. Don Vicente is pardoned for raising arms against the King. Don Vicente begs Violante's forgiveness for his error in attempting to avenge an honor that was lost only in his imagination.

A Thematic Study of the Plot

The profusion of subordinate themes at first makes it difficult to determine which is the principal theme of *Gustos y disgustos son no más que imaginación.* In the bewildering mélange of thematic material, infidelity and honor stand out among the variety of themes introduced. However, when it becomes evident to the protagonist, Don Vicente, that Violante's infidelity exists only in his mind, one realizes that since adultery does not take place, his dishonor is nonexistent. Thus, in the final analysis, the main theme of the drama is «Thou shalt not covet thy neighbor's wife.»

As the plot develops, minor themes of unrequited love, jealousy, woman-monarch concept, mistrust, and imagination are seen to be inseparably fused with the themes of infidelity and honor in such a way that the exclusion of any one of them would destroy the dramatic unity of the play.

Immediately in the opening scene, the audience is plunged *in medias res* into the theme that will carry the action during the first part of Act I, i.e., the Queen's gnawing anxiety of unrequited love. Providing the first hint of the conflict is Violante as she confides to Elvira:

> No me espanto de que así
> llore, Elvira, y se entristezca,
> mirándose aborrecida
> del Rey.
>
> (43-46)[2]

Rapidly following this, Doña María herself provides more information that serves to sharpen our knowledge of her unhappiness at being loathed by the man she loves. This is accomplished as she relates her dream to Violante and Elvira. In the dream, instead of being despised by the King Don Pedro she is very much loved by him and she gives birth to Don Jaime el Conquistador.

By the time the King makes his entrance we are already aware of the conflict existing between him and the Queen. Having fallen from his horse, Don Pedro is brought to Doña María's chambers. As Violante lends assistance in making the unconscious King comfortable, we are not yet aware of the significance of the words that Don Vicente directs to her with a stinging tone of sarcasm: «Qué piadosa estás, Violante» (177). Nor do

[2] The numbers in parentheses following each quoted passage refer to verse numbers in the critical edition.

we fully understand Violante's retort to his biting comment: «Piadosa no, sino cuerda» (178). Very subtly, thus, the theme of jealousy is introduced. Only a faint suggestion is allowed to appear. In fact, so subtle is its presence that it could almost go unnoticed because additional dialogue is immediately interjected to amplify the theme of unrequited love.

Regaining consciousness, the King's remarks confirm what the Queen had lamented earlier and the theme of unrequited love is unequivocally restated:

¿Qué es lo que miro? No puede
haber sido dicha ésta,
puesto que he llegado adonde
lo que más me cansa vea.
(185-188)

In a long soliloquy, Doña María then goes on to reveal the events leading up to the existing state of conjugal affairs. The marriage was a political one effected as a means of establishing peace between the crowns of Aragon and Navarra. Responsible for this marriage was Doña María's father, Count of Montpellier and vassal to the King Don Pedro. The Queen begins to relate the circumstances of the marriage:

Cuando Aragón y Navarra
de duras lides sangrientas
aventuraban las dos
Coronas, fue conveniencia
del Conde de Mompeller,
mi padre ...
(225-230)

Disdainfully Don Pedro interrupts her discourse; obviously the truths she speaks make him uncomfortable. However, Doña María nimbly side-steps the King's scornful words of reprimand and draws her discussion back to the original topic:

> Y volviendo a mi discurso,
> digo que fue conveniencia
> del Conde de Mompeller,
> mi padre, que en esta guerra
> árbitro neutral, podría
> dar la victoria a cualquiera,
> que vos casaseis conmigo,
> y que entonces su prudencia
> aseguraría las paces.
> Quísoos cumplir la promesa;
> casasteis conmigo pues,
> y desde la hora primera,
> que en vuestra corte me visteis,
> o fue rigor de mi estrella,
> o fue envidia de mis desdichas,
> o fue en mis hados fuerza,
> me aborrecisteis de suerte,
> (249-265)

Finishing her soliloquy, the Queen kneels at her husband's feet, begging him to grant her permission to live in a convent. In his usual, disdainful manner, the King refuses her request, adding that the villa, Miravalle, is an adequate convent.

The same deft touch, used to introduce the theme of jealousy is employed to introduce the theme of infidelity. As Don Pedro regains consciousness he fleetingly addresses Violante; his words vaguely suggest the possibility that he feels as much desire for Violante as he feels loathing for his wife:

> Ya no puede ser desdicha
> la mía, puesto que llega
> donde tu crueldad, Violante,
> de mi mal se compadezca.
> (191-194)

Shortly thereafter, as Don Guillén reports to the King that the arrangements with the servant have been made to visit Violante, Don Pedro's aside reveals his inner feelings, establishing firmly the theme of would-be infidelity, albeit only on the part of the King:

> (¡Ha, bellísima Violante,
> qué de pesares me cuestas!
> pero pues mi amor no basta,
> yo me valdré de la fuerza.)
> (309-312)

It is not until after the departure of the King and Queen that the theme of jealousy is introduced again. Once more, Don Vicente chides Violante for the attention which Don Pedro paid to her: «Estarás con los extremos del Rey muy vana y soberbia» (317-318). Her response suggests to the audience that the two have something more than just a speaking acquaintance at court: «Quien no me ve cuando puede, / no me hable cuando se arriesga» (319-320). That jealousy was the force that earlier moved Don Vicente to reproach Violante becomes evident as he confides to his lackey that the King adores Violante in spite of the fact that she already is secretly betrothed to him. Before the end of Act I, the two themes that will be principally responsible for moving the action throughout the play are introduced—jealousy and honor. Chocolate, the *gracioso*, summarizes the situation very appropriately in the answer to his master's lament:

> En efecto, ¡no ha de haber
> amor que, como en comedia,
> lances de celos y honor
> a cada paso no tenga!
> (371-374)

As the action switches to the household of Count Monforte, another form of infidelity is seen to exist—treason. The arrangement with the *criada* to which Don Guillén had alluded earlier is in fact the bribing of Violante's *dueña,* Leonor. The latter finds herself in a quandary, torn between duty to her *ama* and service to the King. Influenced by the 2,000 escudos given her by the King, Leonor chooses to betray her mistress. By this deed infidelity is seen to gain thematic significance in the drama. It is noteworthy that in her debate about whether to serve the interests of Don Vicente or to serve those of the King, Leonor rationalizes her decision on a very material basis:

> Dos años ha que he velado
> de balde las noches frías;
> y el Rey en solos dos días,
> dos mil escudos me ha dado.
> Pues ¡aquí del discurrir!
> ¿No es mejor, quién lo dudó,
> dormir y tomar, que no
> no tomar y no dormir?
> (465-472)

One of the hallmarks of Calderón's style is the intertwining of several minor themes to supplement the main one, a device which helps to further the intrigue and the complication of the plot. In Act I it is not surprising to see the introduction of still another theme, that of mistrust, as an additional complicating element. Count Monforte makes manifest his feeling of mistrust for Don Vicente upon taking leave from the royal villa; he admonishes him for attempting to accompany Violante in their departure. Since Calderón is noted for the device of feeding information piecemeal to the audience, it is not quite clear why at this time the Conde utters to Don Vicente:

tengo por opinión cuerda,
sin que puedan confundirse
en ningún tiempo las señas,
que el amigo y enemigo
lo sean, y lo parezcan .
(342-346)

Count Monforte is unwaningly resolute in keeping Don Vicente as his enemy, and an enemy, by extension, is one who is not to be trusted. A more ample explanation of the Conde's feelings is presented a short time later as he expresses to his daughter his strong disapproval of Don Vicente. By inference he forbids Violante ever to see him again:

que no ha de tener conmigo
mi enemigo bizarrías.
Mío su padre lo fue,
porque en la composición
de Navarra y Aragón
siempre mi opuesto le hallé;
y siendo así que él [Vicente] es quien
heredó rencor igual,
quiero, pues le quiero mal,
que no ande conmigo bien.
(519-528)

This feeling of enmity and mistrust that Count Monforte harbors for Don Vicente becomes a key factor that prevents Violante from disclosing her secret betrothal, creating the opportunity for the King to pursue her favor, and causing Don Vicente to become jealous.

Though the theme of jealousy has been subtly introduced before, it comes into sharp focus in the garden scene that night when Don Vicente pays a secret visit to his betrothed. His reproach to her sums up his feelings:

pues te turban tus rigores,
no será justo que ignores
que tiene en tales desvelos
licencia de pedir celos
marido que da temores.
(707-711)

The King's unexpected appearance on the scene momentarily causes Don Vicente to believe that his jealousy is justified. Later, when he discovers that Don Pedro's presence was not spurred on by Violante, his feelings are allayed. Having been left alone with the Conde to explain the presence of both the King and himself, Don Vicente divulges a secret that Violante and he have kept for two years. It is at this point that the theme of honor is introduced. In accordance with the seventeenth-century code of honor, Don Vicente and Count Monforte share the common plight of dishonor, the former by assuming the role of the *marido ultrajado,* the latter by allowing dishonor to stain his family name. Taking the Conde into his confidence, Don Vicente makes a friend of an enemy as he points out to him:

pues en un propio navío
corriendo tormenta están
juntos hoy tu honor y el mío;
y no has de escapar el tuyo
del no esperado bajío
sin el mío, pues ya son
mi honor y el tuyo uno mismo.
(951-957)

Although Count Monforte regrets having to marry his daughter to the man whom he formerly considered an enemy, he knows that he would regret even more the loss of his cherished honor. Stated differently, Count Monforte is willing to accept the lesser of two evils. Thus, at the end of Act I most of the themes that are to play an important role in the development of the plot have been introduced—Doña María's unrequited love, Don Pedro's intended infidelity to her, Don Vicente's jealousy, and the impending peril of dishonor that Count Monforte shares with his former enemy.

Act II opens with a conversation between Don Pedro and Don Guillén, his confidant. The former expresses sentiments of regret at the unfortunate turn of events of the previous night. Infidelity being a significant element in the play, it is important to note that Don Guillén represents the theme in reverse: for better or for worse, Don Guillén is truly faithful to the King. Don Pedro confesses the enormity of his love for Violante and his jealousy about her. For a fleeting moment, nevertheless, the King ostensibly shows a small measure of compassion for Don Vicente, avowing that he was indeed remiss in leaving the Conde and Don Vicente under such trying circumstances, for neither was Violante and Don Vicente's marriage officially sanctioned, nor was the Conde's feud with Don Vicente settled:

> que fue muy imprudente
> acción dejar allí dos enemigos
> sin terceros, ni medios, ni testigos,
> tan ciegos, tan confusos, tan turbados,
> (1079-1082)

However, once alone with Don Guillén and having granted permission to Count Monforte to give Violante in marriage to Don Vicente, the King does an about-face in his benevolence: he confides to Don Guillén his intentions of continuing his courtship of Violante. In spite of Don Guillén's attempts to dissuade him from following this dishonorable cource of action, Don Pedro obstinately refuses sound advice. One wonders at this moment at the sincerity of his previously expressed regrets.

An interesting parallel becomes conspicuously evident as Don Pedro expounds on the reasons for his change of heart. One is reminded of Leonor in Act I as she rationalized her deed of infidelity to Violante. The servant's reasoning was based on material gain; the King's reasoning on loftier ideals:

> De hacer algún bien, es tal
> la alabanza, Don Guillén,
> que haciendo uno ajeno bien,
> no siente su propio mal;
> pues por consuelo se queda
> lo bien que procede allí.
> Luego en este caso, a mí,
> no hay elección mía que pueda
> dejarme a mí satisfecho
> de que yo lo hice, pues
> ellos lo han hecho, y no es
> consuelo el verlo ya hecho;
> y así postrado y rendido,
> no hallo medio a mi dolor.
> (1204-1217)

Although his plea has a convincing ring, one is left with the conviction that he is only absolving himself for an action that he knows is in essence dishonorable. In casting aside his original intentions, the King once more brings in the theme of infidelity. In his reversal Don Pedro betrays not only the Conde and Don Vicente but also his own integrity and honor as a gentleman and a monarch.

In the following scene, attempting to console her mistress, Leonor is again untrue to Violante. The servant declares that although she is not an accomplice to her mistress' unhappiness, she would like to be instrumental in consoling. Unbeknown to Violante, her *dueña* has had a hand in the events that have brought her grief.

In expressing woe at her father's mysterious conduct, Violante introduces the theme of mistrust for the second time. It is with great skepticism that she interprets her father's actions which occur following his encounter with the two men in the garden. Being absent from the conversation that ensued between her father and her fiancé, seeing the Conde utter not a word as he locked himself in his room after Don Vicente's departure, and knowing that Count Monforte left early in the morning without a word of explanation, Violante's reaction is to mistrust. Her only surmise is that her father is seeking a means of punishing her: «...Porque / el que disimulos hace / a su enojo, y no le riñe, / es que trata de vengarse» (1306-1309).

Distrust continues to pervade the atmosphere as Count Monforte arrives with Don Vicente to announce to Violante the good news of the marriage. Persevering in her original thesis, she anticipates her father's words while attempting to mouth an explanation in her defense. Even after hearing the Conde's announcement of his knowledge of her secret betrothal and of his intentions to sanction the marriage, Violante is loath to trust her father, believing him to be employing trickery to make her confess to her disobedience:

> (Él solicita
> con este engaño informarse
> de la verdad de mi amor,
> y le ha de salir en balde...)
> (1432-1435)

Fear of confirming her father's suspicions occasions Violante's answer that she would never marry Don Vicente, even if the refusal would mean her death. This retort evokes distrust not only from her fiancé, who is within earshot of the conversation, but also from her father. In an aside, Count Monforte doubts for an instant Don Vicente's sincerity, wondering if the latter did not in fact invent the story of the secret betrothal in order to trick the Conde into making peace with him. Unaware of Violante's reasoning, Don Vicente, too, begins to doubt his fiancée's true feelings. Since the King has already granted permission for the marriage, Count Monforte feels impelled to proceed with the plan. For the moment at least, the Conde's decision to sanction the marriage, helps to allay all feelings of mistrust on the part of all three persons.

With the arrival of Don Guillén bearing the two letters addressed to the newlyweds, the theme of mistrust emerges again as Don Vicente exclaims in an aside: «Cuidado, penas, que viene / envuelto en flores el áspid» (1574-1575). Don Vicente's suspicions are not ill-founded, for although the King's letters bear good news, they also announce the device which Don Pedro is employing in order to remove the obstacle that prevents him from freely paying court to Violante.

Distrust as a theme continues to dominate the action as Don Vicente is making ready to depart on his mission in behalf of the Crown, and as Violante is asking for permission to remain with the Queen during his absence. Don Vicente accedes to his wife's wishes, but makes a request of his own. It is reasonable to believe that although he may be sincere in his request, Don Vicente has other reasons for asking his wife to give a false excuse for wanting to remain with Doña María. Don Vicente may not wish people at court to think that he mistrusts his wife alone in her father's house. He, therefore, asks Violante to give as pretext the non-existent ill will that the Conde harbors for being forced to marry his daughter to his former enemy. Ironically, it is because Violante stays with the Queen that Don Vicente is to suffer the anguish of jealousy and supposed dishonor. The theme of mistrust spills over into the following scene as Count Monforte is informed by Doña María that she wishes to have his daughter remain at the villa until the return of Don Vicente. Not being aware that it was Violante who instigated the request, the Conde interprets Doña María's gesture to be motivated by jealousy and mistrust:

> ¡Dichosa ella [Violante] que ha podido
> conocer tanto favor!
> ¡Y desdichado mi honor,
> pues a término ha venido,
> que la Reina, sospechosa
> del Rey y Violante bella,
> quiera asegurarse della,
> honrándola de celosa!
>
> (1788-1795)

Paralleling Count Monforte's sentiments are those of Don Guillén in the next scene. That evening as he accompanies Don Pedro in his intended clandestine rendezvous with Violante, Don Guillén reports to the King that she is not returning home with her father. Learning that it has been Doña María who asked that Violante stay with her, Don Guillén interjects his personal evaluation of the Queen's motives:

> De que claro he conocido
> que está de Violante bella
> la Reina celosa, o que
> recatada y temerosa
> de sí está Violante hermosa;
>
> (1834-1838)

Jealousy and mistrust thus continue to be the important themes carrying the action of Act II. Is is astonishing that both men should draw the same conclusion. The small ounce of truth contained in their judgments, ironically, will eventually prove to carry more weight than is surmised.

Mistaking the Queen for Violante in the darkness of the balcony window, the King continues the conversation that he had originally started with Violante. Doña María experiences her first pangs of jealousy when her husband speaks amorously to her, addressing her as Violante. She utters in an aside:

> (A mi fortuna cruel
> sólo celos le faltaban
> de sentir y padecer.
> Ya está cabal el dolor.)
> (2011-2014)

Jealousy also grips Don Vicente once more as he and Chocolate approach the balcony and observe the unidentifiable figure of the King conversing through the window. Wishing to satisfy his suspicion without a witness, Don Vicente sends his lackey away; his exclamation of woe: «¡Qué fuera, válgame el cielo, / que este hombre fuera el Rey!» (2082-2083), clearly expresses his feeling of utter suspicion.

Toward the end of Act II the *reina-mujer* conflict is introduced as Doña María resolves to continue her masquerade as Violante, hoping to win the love of the King. Although she is a Queen, she is also a woman and she is determined to win him, even by deceit if need be. In her resolution, the *mujer* instinct overpowers the *reina* sense of duty.

Act II ends on a note of suspense as the theme of honor reaches a high degree of importance. As Don Vicente approaches the balcony for the second time, Don Pedro is joyfully departing, having been granted permission by the Queen to visit her freely. Taking the shadowy figure of Don Vicente to be Don Guillén, the King exclaims to him that Violante has agreed to a rendezvous. When Don Pedro realizes that he has confided his secret to the wrong man, he runs in pursuit, anxious to know to whom he has divulged his secret. Don Vicente's unwillingness to reveal his identity makes him flee. At this point his suspicion of his wife's infidelity with the King is confirmed, but his predicament is complicated by the fact that a person of royal blood has offended his honor. His only defense, then, is to flee, and Don Vicente goes to war believing that Violante is dishonoring him.

Although most of Act III is devoted to developing the honor theme, the queen-woman theme is still an important motivating element of the plot, for it is apparent that the Queen has continued her rendezvous with the King at the window. The great perturbation of Don Pedro, however, at not having uncovered the identity of the strange man whom he had pursued, has a strong link with the honor theme.

The Queen receives the news of Don Vicente's imminent return. The King suggests the possibility of continuing their meetings in her own home after the return of her husband. Doña María at this point realizes that the end of the masquerade is near and provides for the prevention of her discovery by informing Don Pedro that she will no longer see him and will in fact deny forever this very conversation and all other rendezvous. The theme of infidelity and hishonor reaches a pinnacle in the King's request:

> pero ya, si sois de uno,
> ¿no podrá el ciego dios
> que seamos dichosos dos?
> (2308-2310)

He is totally unaware of the irony in his words when he alludes to the possibility of becoming the Queen's lover.

The Queen, who is speaking as Violante, realizes the impossibility of such an arrangement, and couches her reply in words that prevent the compromise of her indentity:

> Fuera no serlo ninguno,
> porque el querer y reinar
> no ha de partirse.
> (2311-2313)

The capture of Chocolate and the extraction of the information of his master's premature return from Mallorca, places the honor theme in sharp relief, for the King is now well aware that the mysterious man who appeared in the garden is indeed Don Vicente. His early return gives convincing evidence that he is bent on avenging his honor, feeling *ultrajado* by the King. This being the case, Don Pedro feels compelled to warn Violante that her life is in danger. Honor, then, becomes the underlying theme that heightens the action to a rapid pace in the remaining part of Act III.

Finding Chocolate after his encounter with both the King and Don Guillén, Don Vicente is deceived by his lackey. Chocolate denies having informed the King of his return. Don Vicente becomes the victim of his lackey's treason, in much the same way in which Violante suffered from her servant in Act I.

Again feelings of doubt and mistrust overwhelm Don Vicente when he recalls the events that have occurred. It is important to note that the word *imaginación,* the axis on which the plot of Act III revolves, is mentioned for the first time in the play:

> ¡Válgame Dios! ¿Qué he de hacer,
> cercado de tan crueles
> imaginaciones locas
> como a mi discurso ofenden?
> (2575-2578)

Clearly then, this is a crucial moment in the drama, for imagination becomes an inseparable counterpart of the honor theme. Don Vicente admits to himself that imagination is what plagues his mind. It is responsible for his feeling of mistrust and jealousy of Violante as well as for his fear of dishonor. Imagination becomes ever more important as Don Vicente reviews the incidents in his mind: First, before leaving for Mallorca he discovered the King at the window; second, upon encountering the King he heard his confession of winning Violante's favor; third, after returning from his campaign he found Don Guillén at the window. Realizing that imagination is responsible for his disquiet, Don Vicente struggles to keep an open mind and to suppress judgment until he has more conclusive proof of infidelity. It is for this reason that he exclaims:

> Mas ¿qué digo, indicio? Miento;
> que aún el indicio más leve
> no ha llegado a mi noticia.
> Miente mi discurso, miente
> mi imaginación, ...
> ....
> Haz, honor, que aquesta loca
> imaginación me deje.
> (2611-2624)

In confiding to Elvira the event of being mistaken for Violante by the King, the Queen reiterates the theme of her unrequited love; here for the second time, the word imagination assumes importance. Masquerading as she did in order to ascertain the degree of involvement between Violante and Don Pedro, the Queen well realizes that she is playing upon the King's imagination in order to open his eyes to her merits as a woman:

Luego si yo con fingir
que soy la que adora, tengo
su imaginación burlada,
parado su pensamiento,
mi respeto asegurado,
pacíficos mis recelos,
no ha sido culpable, Elvira,
de todo mi fingimiento.
(2685-2692)

Don Vicente's eagerness to have proof that his dishonor exists only in his imagination prompts him to see Violante before officially reporting to the King. In the ensuing scene he vacillates between trust and doubts. Despite his attempt to feign joy and serenity on meeting his wife, Violante discerns the disquiet that pervades his countenance and manner. Observing the concern which Violante shows for his lukewarm greeting, Don Vicente asks himself if her manner could possibly be a sham. His mistrust gradually wanes when he allows himself now to trust his senses as he looks upon Violante rather than to rely upon the memory of what he once saw. Violante's tears allay his doubts and lead him to question his imagination as he utters in an aside:

(Aora es tiempo, aora,
ilusión mal nacida,
de darte por vencida.
Violante es la que llora;
no dirás más verdad, ¿qué estoy dudando?
imaginando tú, y ella llorando.)
(2807-2812)

The couple's renewed happiness is short-lived, for their joyous and tearful embraces are interrupted by Leonor who excitedly informs them of the arrival of the King at the villa. Having convinced himself that all is well with Violante and himself, Don Vicente's immediate reaction is to accept the King's arrival at his own villa as a very logical act. When Leonor adds that he is coming there directly and not to the Queen's chambers, it is Violante who is quick to explain the logic behind the King's act, namely his desire to avoid his wife whom he detests. Don Vicente's feelings of mistrust fire up again, as he comments to Violante:

> Pues no extrañas
> tan gran visita, no dudo
> que esto muchas veces pasa.
> (2856-2858)

At her denial of such visits, Don Vicente rationalizes his outburst as fear of being discovered there before officially reporting to court. In his allegation he is, of course, covering up for his real sentiment of mistrust and rage and is deceiving no one but himself.

As Don Pedro enters the room, Don Vicente and Chocolate hide. This hiding to avoid the King and this eavesdropping to hear his conversation parallel that of Act I. Violante, for her part, welcomes this situation for she hopes that her husband will be convinced of the falseness of his accusations of infidelity. The conversation at first goes well in her favor, as she honestly comments on her surprise at seeing Don Pedro after such a long absence, moreover in her chambers: «cosa a vos tan poco usada, / y en mí tan poco advertida» (2906-2907). Violante starts losing ground when the King makes mention of the fact that her life is in peril. Her denial of having seen Don Vicente confirms Don Pedro's suspicions of her danger. She feels all is lost as the King mentions the mysterious man who interrupted their rendezvous the previous night. Don Pedro then proceeds to caution Violante not to feign innocence, for although in anger she once vowed to deny the Kings favors, this is not the time to keep her word.

The more she denies, the more the King shatters the credibility of her innocence.

The action reaches a crisis at this moment at a time when all minor themes become strongly integrated to support the main themes. Mistrust, treason, deception, jealousy, unrequited love, and imagination bring infidelity and honor into sharp relief. Because of the enmity and mistrust which Count Monforte harbored for Don Vicente, his daughter, Violante, was unwilling to disclose her secret betrothal. Not knowing of the betrothal led Don Pedro to fancy himself a pretender to Violante's affections, aided in his endeavor by Leonor's treasonable act. The King's attentions to Violante precipitated Don Vicente's jealousy. Moreover, his volatile imagination has led him to suspect his wife of infidelity and consequently to believe himself a dishonored man. Meanwhile, the Queen has now become not only the victim of unrequited love, but also has fallen into the anguish of jealousy.

When Doña María appears, Don Pedro deceives her by telling her that he mistook Violante's room for hers. Being aware of her husband's affection for Violante, the Queen chides her consort with these words that carry thematic significance: «y ya, señor, que os engaña / la imaginación, pues ciega / a unas busca y a otras halla» (3004-3006). She adds shortly afterward:

> (¡Quién creyera,
> que una imaginación haga
> que se aborrezca de día
> lo que de noche se ama!)
> (3017-3020)

Don Vicente, now firmly convinced of his dishonor, is resolved that his wife must die for her infidelity. Just as he is about to emerge from hiding with dagger in hand, the Queen, wishing to prevent Violante from remaining alone with Don Guillén, beckons her and thus suspends her execution. The crisis has passed.

Alone now, Don Vicente ponders his dilemma. In accordance with the seventeenth-century code of honor, he is justified in taking revenge, slaying those who would dishonor him. But, Don Pedro is the man responsible for his grievance and he may not take up arms against the King. For that reason he says: «y pues no puedo tomar / más de la media venganza» (3067-3068). Violante is aware not only of her impending fate but also her dilemma of returning or not returning to her room:

> si temerosa me ausento,
> añado otro fundamento.
> Ir es desesperación;
> no ir, confirmar traición.
> (3116-3119)

In her anxiety, she alludes to the injustice to which the woman is subjected under the strict code of honor. She hits on the nerve center of the questionable logic of the code, as she pleas:

> Razón tengo ... no equivale;
> pues si no hay cosa que iguale,
> ¿qué importa tener razón?
> (3120-3122)

Finding his distraught daughter, Count Monforte helps her in her predicament. He is prepared, reassured of her innocence, to defend her as they both go to find Don Vicente.

In the last scene, as Don Pedro and Don Vicente make their way to the window in the garden, each has his own motive in mind: the former to win her favor;

the latter to kill her. Meanwhile Doña María realizes the time has come to make her identity known to the King. Just before her appearance at the window, she instructs Elvira to stand by to bring the lantern in the event of being summoned. Coming to the window, the Queen once more alludes to the *reina-mujer* concept and again attributes her actions to the *mujer* in her:

> pues cuantas a sus esposos
> los quisieren como yo,
> procurarán divertirles
> de cualquier ajeno amor.
> El ser Reina en este caso
> será pequeña objeción;
> que amor es alma, y las almas
> Reinas, no vasallas son.
> (3279-3286)

The drama approaches its climax as protagonist and antagonist arrive at the window. Sensing each other's presence, but in the dark unable to recognize each other, Don Vicente and the King take swords in hand. Don Pedro is prepared to defend the woman whom he believes to be Violante. As Don Vicente prepares to fight, he exclaims: «Sed testigos, cielos, que / tiro a Violante, al Rey no» (3315-3316). At Don Vicente's shouting, all run to the scene with Elvira carrying a lantern. The light shining on all characters dramatically and symbolically signals the climax to the action. Seeing that it is the King whom he was fighting, Don Vicente begs forgiveness. Don Pedro realizes that the woman behind the window is not Violante but rather his own wife. The misunderstanding is cleared up with the Queen explaining to her husband:

> Con el nombre de Violante
> os hablé por el balcón.

De mí estáis enamorado
de noche, si de día no.
Pues una mentira, Rey,
tanta pasión os debió,
¿por qué una verdad no puede
deber la misma pasión?
(3335-3342)

Doña María continues her discourse in hope of convincing the King of his error. In her arguments she attributes the cause of all misunderstanding to imagination, the same imagination that once gave the King pleasure while giving grief to Don Vicente.

The denouement follows rapidly as the King forgives the Queen for her deception and adds that he regrets having loved her as another woman rather than having loved her for herself. Don Pedro also makes peace with Don Vicente who, in turn, begs Violante's forgiveness for having doubted her fidelity. Chocolate restates the main theme of the play as he interjects:

Ésta es verdadera historia,
de que saque el pío lector,
que se estime lo que es propio;
que lo ajeno no es mejor.
Pues como imagina un hombre,
que todas mujeres son,
y que no es mejor ninguna,
porque cualquiera es peor,
con la suya vivirá
contento. Pues lo enseñó
la comedia, ...
(3413-3423)

Characterization

Since the thematic common denominator of the play is honor (and by extension, infidelity), of necessity each of the principal characters must be considered in the light of the role which he plays in the development of the main theme. Since the *comedia* reflects society and its ideologies, to appreciate the present play it is necessary to understand an important facet of the culture of the seventeenth century, the point of honor *(pundonor)* and its social ramifications. The Spaniard of the seventeenth century possessed a strong feeling of self-esteem which was accompanied by a desire to be respected. The end result of these feelings is *honor*, the dignity of the individual or his reputation in the community. Everett W. Hesse sums up the social phenomenon in these words:

> The problem of honor is a psychological one and has its roots deep in the human personality. For this reason it has had a tradition that reaches back in the remote past and extends down to our own day under variant guises in different parts of the world as «saving-face» or «reputation» or personal and family integrity. What will other people say about us if we are caught in a compromising situation and made the laughing-stock of the community?[3]

A detailed analysis of the main characters will follow a brief sketch of each individual. The initial discussion of the characters places each in proper perspective with regard to the role that he plays in the theme of honor. On the following page the diagram schematically shows the relationships existing between characters. It can readily be seen that the relationship between Don Vicente, Don Pedro, and Violante evolves into a triangle. At one tip of the triangle is Don Vicente, the protagonist. His love for Violante is reciprocated by the heroine. Occupying another tip of the triangle is the King Don

---

[3] CALDERÓN DE LA BARCA (New York: Twayne Publishers, Inc., 1967), p. 118.

DIAGRAM OF CHARACTER RELATIONSHIPS

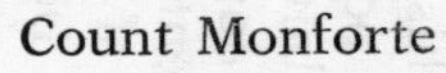

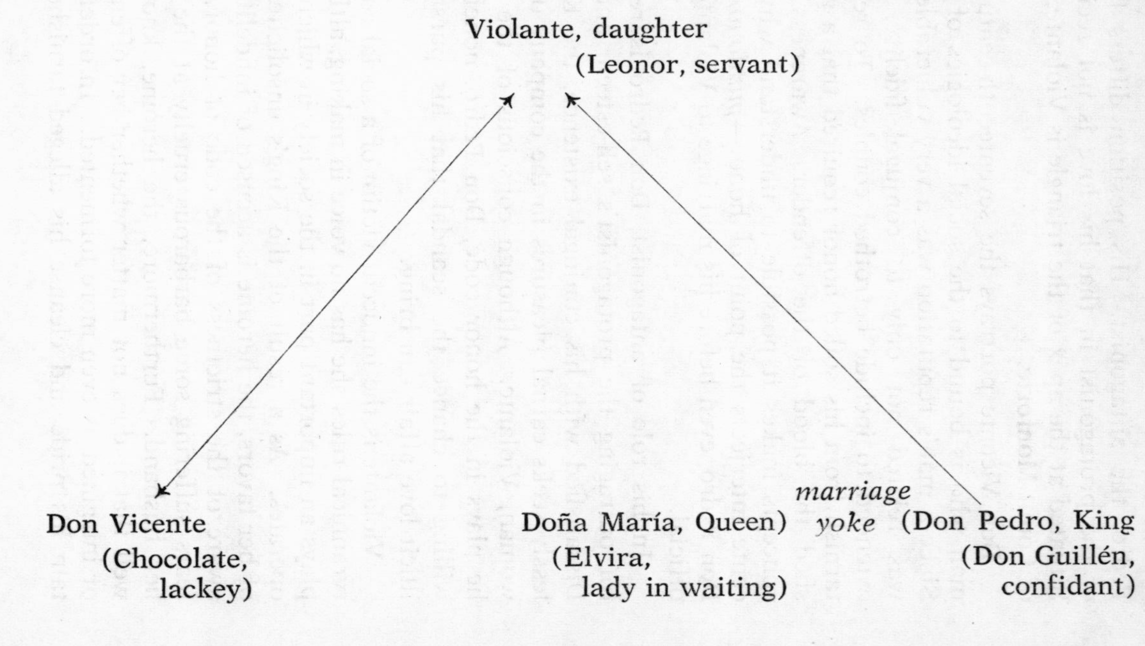

Pedro, the antagonist. His position differs from that of the protagonist in that his love is not reciprocated. Situated at the apex of the triangle is Violante, daughter of Count Monforte.

Don Vicente portrays the seventeenth-century gentleman who is bound to the social ideologies of his time. Since a man's reputation was a very vulnerable point, it was related not only to conjugal fidelity, but also extended to include betrothed couples. To remove the tarnish from his soiled honor required that a gentleman shed the blood of the offender. Awareness of these concepts makes it possible to understand why Don Vicente interjects the point of honor—*pundonor*—against Don Pedro, even before his marriage to Violante is made official.

In his role of antagonist, Don Pedro is responsible for outraging the protagonist's self-esteem and dignity. Dissatisfied with his conjugal existence, the King recklessly seeks carnal pleasures in the company of another woman, Violante. Although conscious of the role that he plays in the honor code, Don Pedro, nonetheless, is willing to chance the scandal that his pursuit of an illicit love affair can bring.

Violante is the innocent victim of a social code whose tyrannical rules she has no voice in making, although she plays an important part in the society in which the code operates. As a result of the King's unsolicited pursuit of her favors, the heroine is accused of infidelity. Being aware of the strictness of the code of honor, Violante fears suffering some barbarous cruelty at the hands of her husband. Furthermore, the heroine, knowing full well that it does not matter whether her offense is real or imagined, is even more tormented. In order to maintain his pride and cleanse his alleged tarnished honor, her husband is permitted to kill her even though the infidelity is merely suspected and not proven.

Count Monforte also plays an important role as the custodian of his daughter's honor. «All male members of a household were responsible for protecting the family's name, and no honorable gentleman could leave family dishonor unavenged.»[4] Realizing the importance of his responsibility, the Conde is easily convinced of the grave necessity of joining forces with Don Vicente in order to save the family honor which mere gossip may sully. Count Monforte, moreover, puts into practice the seventeenth-century philosophy that it does not matter whether a woman loves the man she marries or that she finds happiness with him. What is most important is to give his daughter the status of a married woman, once the possibility of gossip has been established. It is for this reason that the Conde is determined to proceed with his plan to marry Violante to Don Vicente even when she momentarily denies loving him.

The Queen Doña María complicates the love triangle. Quite by chance she becomes aware of the relationship which her husband is seeking to establish with Violante. There is no one to whom the Queen can appeal for help since the one person responsible for her affront is the King himself, and no one is higher than the King. In the end, the Queen herself is the one who holds the key to the resolution of the conflict that develops.

Each of the remaining characters is paired off with one of the main characters for the mutual exchange of confidential problems. Chocolate, the *gracioso,* plays the dual role of buffoon and confidant to Don Vicente. Most of the time his function is to supply comedy relief to the

[4] Richard E. CHANDLER and Kessel SCHWARTZ, *A New History of Spanish Literature* (Baton Rouge: Louisiana State University Press, 1961), p. 92.

play, but at rare moments he gives evidence of possessing the qualities of a sage adviser. Don Guillén serves as the King's adviser and confidant. Fulfilling the duties of a lady in waiting, Elvira serves as confidante to the Queen. Leonor, *dueña* to Violante, also plays the role of counselor and confidante.

In order to have a better understanding of the characters, it is necessary to study each one from the following points of view: First, from the point of view of the image which the character projects of himself to the viewer, by word and deed; second, from the point of view of those people surrounding the character within the play. Since no physical description is in evidence throughout the play, this twofold approach is important in formulating opinions of the *dramatis personae.* The discussion will be limited to the four main characters who are responsible for carrying the action in the play: the King, the Queen, Don Vicente, and Violante.

In the opening scene of Act I Don Pedro projects himself as a fearless man. Despite the fact that he has just suffered a serious and dangerous fall from his horse, he insists on mounting the beast again. Addressing his confidant he orders:

> Don Guillén, dadme un caballo,
> o el mismo, porque no entienda
> que a mí me puede poner
> temor ninguna soberbia.
>
> (199-202)

Determined to be admitted to Violante's graces the King shows forcefulness and self-assuredness. Only a hint of his overbearing character is discernible at first. Departing from the royal villa after his verbal encounter with the Queen, Don Pedro utters in an aside:

(¡Ha, bellísima Violante,
qué de pesares me cuestas!
pero pues mi amor no basta,
yo me valdré de la fuerza.)
(309-312)

Toward the end of Act I, after scaling the wall to pay his clandestine visit to Violante in the household of Count Monforte, the King demonstrates not only his audacious nature but also his braggadocio:

No diga que tiene amor
quien no tiene atrevimiento.
(734-735)

¿Quién creerá que mi valor
tiene a una mujer temor?
(783-784)

Seeing that his ardent declaration of love is not favorably received, the King's tenacity and arrogance become more evident:

...y no
volveré atrás, porque yo
soy a un tiempo Rey y amante
(797-799)

después que turbada os vi,
nada os defiende de mí;
(817-818)

His attempt to woo Violante having ended in a fiasco, Don Pedro's conversation with Don Guillén in Act II the following morning gives superficial indication of a change of heart and true repentance. His arguments sound so convincing that they have a ring of sincerity:

> Mi dolor a esas causas corresponde,
> y entre tantos desvelos,
> con ser tanto mi amor, tantos mis celos,
> si de todo pudiera
> enmendar algo al lance, sólo fuera
> el haberme ausentado
> de allí sin que quedara afetuado
> el casamiento y paz de Don Vicente
> con el Conde;
>
> (1071-1079)

Once Count Monforte and Don Vicente depart, and once they have received the King's blessings on the marriage, Don Pedro declares his true intentions of continuing to pursue Violante. By this declaration, the monarch shows still another flaw in his character—deceitfulness.

It is not until Act III that the King displays any qualities that are indicative of a warm, compassionate human being. First, believing that he has compromised a married woman's honor, he takes steps to protect her from the wrath of an outraged husband. He warns Violante of Don Vicente's early return. Second, at play's end he is willing to forgive Doña María's deception, acknowledge her virtues, accept her as his wife, forgive Don Vicente for taking up arms against him, and beg forgiveness of Violante for the grief that he caused her.

Other characters who project feelings about Don Pedro are Violante and Doña María. Arriving at the villa when the play opens, Violante converses with Elvira and alludes to the Queen's unhappiness which is caused by the King. The first mention of the King's name is accompanied by the unflattering adjective of *cruel*. Linking Don Pedro's name to that of Pedro el Cruel, the King's image by innuendo gains the same notoriety:

> Mas la condición del Rey
> es terrible. Todos cuentan

crueldades suyas. Parece
que el nombre de Pedro lleva
estas desdichas tras sí;
pues tres Pedros...
(49-54)

In a later scene, Doña María, recalling the history of her marriage to Don Pedro and her subsequent ill treatment at the hands of her husband, also helps in establishing the King's image. The King himself adds to the antipathy of his character by his cruel and persistently disdainful regard for the Queen. She alludes to his ill treatment in the long discourse in Act I, a portion of which is cited here:

casasteis conmigo pues,
y desde la hora primera
que en vuestra corte me visteis,
....
me aborrecisteis de suerte,
(259-265)

From the foregoing analysis, it can be concluded that the most lingering aspect in the characterization of the King Don Pedro is that of the playboy king. In this role, he embodies many of the qualities of the ideal seventeenth-century *caballero*. He is adventurous, daring, fearless, proud, and self-assured. Nevertheless, he is arrogant and overbearing, and it is those facets of his character that almost bring tragedy to his life and to the lives of those associated with him.

Let us now consider the characterization of the Queen Doña María. Immediately after the play opens, the audience is suddenly immersed in the mental conflict that engulfs Doña María, when Elvira, the Queen's lady in waiting, alludes to «la pasión de su tristeza» (8). Continuing their conversation, Violante and Elvira provide additional information on the Queen's state of mind:

ELVIRA. Su grande melancolía
en la soledad no cesa.
VIOLANTE. No me espanto de que así
llore, Elvira, y se entristezca.
mirándose aborrecida
del Rey. ¡Qué su gran belleza
con la magestad no basten
a contrastar una estrella!
(41-48)

Key words that stand out in the cited passage and that are functional in depicting the emotional condition of the Queen are: melancholia, solitude, weeping, sadness, and loathing. Calderón allows Doña María to express her own feelings on the torment of being unloved:

¡Qué vana es y qué ligera
la dicha del desdichado,
pues sólo el sueño la engendra!
(62-64)

Ostensibly, to the Queen, happiness is a shallow and fleeting illusion that only dreams can engender. Not finding fulfillment of the love for which she yearns in her waking hours, her mental affliction is such that she realizes this fulfillment in her dreams:

Soñaba amigas; ¿quién duda
que soñaba, puesto que era
tan gran dicha como hallarme
del Rey adorada? Desta
novedad, tan novedad,
que no espero que acontezca,
era el medianero un hijo
(83-89)

Dreaming becomes an escape mechanism for Doña María, discovering that she finds happiness while sleeping but sadness while awake. It is in this respect that

Calderón masterfully shows extraordinary understanding of human nature and conveys the idea that the son, born to the Queen in her dreams, represents the longed-for catalyst that will awaken the love of her husband and that will ultimately unite him to her.

The image that the Queen projects of herself in the eyes of her husband is totally unfavorable. Don Pedro makes no effort to hide his disaffection for Doña María. Throughout the play, his every remark to her is intended to humiliate and to hurt her. Moreover, all commentary made in reference to the Queen (either in normal dialogue or in asides) is filled with negative sentiments of repulsion, abhorrence, and disdain. An example of one of these invectives is cited below. It occurs early in the play when the King regains consciousness and addresses his wife:

> ¿Qué es lo que miro? No puede
> haber sido dicha ésta,
> puesto que he llegado adonde
> lo que más me cansa vea.
> (185-188)

If at first the Queen projects herself as a helpless, fragile, and highly vulnerable person, it is not long afterward that she has occasion to alter the original opinion held of her. The flashback relating the circumstances of her marriage to Don Pedro provides the opportunity for Doña María to divulge other facets of her character:

> Vasallo mi padre fue;
> pero de tanta nobleza,
> de tanto honor, tanta fama,
> tanto lustre, tantas fuerzas,
> que si hubiera otro en el mundo
> mejor que vos, cosa es cierta;
> que con vos no me casara:

Mirad si es digna respuesta,
pues honro a padre y marido
con sola una razón mesma.
(239-248)

In her discourse the Queen shows that she is an intelligent, level-headed woman with the cunning necessary to deal with a personality as strong as that of the King. By her well-chosen words the Queen is able to honor her father's deeds without violating the respect due her husband. In lauding her father's astuteness and good judgment in having chosen Don Pedro for her spouse, Doña María cunningly flatters her husband assuring him that had there been a better prospect, her father would not have selected Don Pedro for the match. At the end of the Queen's discourse one is able to see not only the sad and melancholy side of her personality, but also those qualities that transform her into a woman of indomitable character.

Although obsessed with the torment of unrequited love, Doña María nevertheless shows strength in her willingness to alleviate her pain when Elvira suggests that she find a cure to her afflictions by surrounding herself with pleasant company, music, and gaiety:

Porque no parezca, Elvira,
que en mí esta necia pasión
es ya desesperación,
aunque el pensarlo me admira,
me reduciré. Di a cuantas
me sirven que al jardín voy,
y que bajen a él.
(1700-1706)

In Act II the Queen's encounter with the King in the garden proves useful in revealing more of her intimate qualities. Discovering that Don Pedro believes her to be

Violante, the Queen assumes the role of the other woman but expresses sincere sentiments that are strictly her own:

> No me juzguéis tan ingrata,
> tan esquiva y tan cruel;
> que no es ser cruel y esquiva
> el ser noble una mujer.
> Basta decir que si fuera
> justo declararme, sé
> que estás hablando, señor,
> con quien os quiere muy bien;
> pero su estrella ha impedido
> el logro de tanta fe.
> (2034-2043)

Her decision to engage in the masquerade clearly shows the overpowering force that compels the woman instinct in Doña María to fight for the man she loves; for, although she is a monarch, she is first a woman. Moreover, if the *mujer* triumphs over the *reina,* feminine guile never supplants honesty. She retains her dignity throughout the masquerade, never stooping to win the King's love by fraud. Employing ingenuity at all times, her words are couched in a manner that allows her to speak truthfully without giving away her true identity. The only deception that exists in her actions is the masquerade itself. So astutely does she play her role that the King later shows signs of attraction more to her intellect than to her beauty, falling in love with the soul rather than the flesh. Unknowingly, Don Pedro has fallen in love with the Queen, although he believes that he is addressing Violante as he says to her:

> Si hermosa os amé, Violante,
> discreta os adoraré;
> que esa hermosura del alma
> me rinde segunda vez.
> (2060-2063)

From the foregoing analysis it can be concluded that the Queen projects herself as a warm and intensely human character. She gains empathy early in the play by being the unfortunate victim of unrequited love. It has been seen, however, that gradually she assumes the dimensions of a strong character. If at first she gives the impression of being a weak and defenseless creature, she undergoes a metamorphosis that ultimately allows her to command respect as an intelligent and courageous woman who is willing to fight for what she holds dear. In the end, Doña María emerges as a much stronger character than Violante, the heroine.

One emotion dominates Don Vicentes actions throughout the play—jealousy. That emotion is the salient feature in his characterization, for in almost every utterance during the first act the protagonist projects the one preoccupation that seems ever present in his thoughts—jealousy of Violante.

In his essay on jealousy as a recurring theme in the Spanish dramas, Hymen Alpern has this opinion to offer on the subject:

> Among the passions portrayed by Spanish dramatic writers of the sixteenth and seventeenth centuries the fury of jealousy is conspicuous. It is a theme which, being closely related to the «pundonor», reflects the national temper of the Spaniard. «Jealous as a Spaniard» is a proverbial simile that finds ample justification in the «comedia.» [5]

As the analysis of Don Vicente's character will disclose, there is evidence in the play supporting the belief that jealousy indeed reflects the national temper of the Spaniard.

---

[5] «Jealousy as a Dramatic Motive in the Spanish 'Comedia'», *The Romanic Review,* XIV (1923), 276.

At first, Don Vicente's remarks only subtly suggest his feelings of jealousy. The audience is not fully aware of the significance of his words when at the beginning of Act I he says to Violante: «Qué piadosa estás, Violante» (177); and later in the same scene: «Estarás con los extremos / del Rey muy vana y soberbia» (317-318). As the plot unfolds, jealousy becomes ever more a powerful force governing the actions of Don Vicente. Before too long, however, a preoccupation with honor becomes inseparably linked with the emotion of jealousy in the mind of the protagonist. This concept first becomes evident to the onlooker when the troubled Don Vicente complains to his lackey of the unhappy state of affairs between Violante and himself:

> Mucho, pues me agravia el uno [King]
> sin que el otro [Violante] me consienta
> poner reparo al agravio
> con mi honor o con mi ausencia.
> (367-370)

Chocolate's rejoinder foreshadows what will dominate his master's thoughts for the remainder of the play:

> En efeto, ¡no ha de haber
> amor que, como en comedia,
> lances de celos y honor
> a cada paso no tenga!
> (371-374)

Many incidents in the beginning of the drama illustrate the jealousy felt by Don Vicente. For example, the scene in which Don Vicente calls on Violante after their harsh exchange of words at the royal villa illustrates the point:

> ...pues los cielos
> saben que si allí vivía,

era porque allá tenía
conmigo todos mis celos.
(589-592)

And later in the same scene when Violante reviews the events of their first meeting and subsequent secret marriage, Don Vicente interrupts her colloquy with these words:

Esto diré yo mejor,
que si callé con amor,
no puedo callar con celos:
(679-681)

It is difficult for Don Vicente to make any remark without uttering the word *celos*. Since he does experience this difficulty, some important questions come to mind about his character: Is he jealous by nature? Would he have been jealous without provocation? Is his jealousy spurred on by his deep-seated fear of dishonor?

Perhaps Lord Holland was correct when, in the nineteenth century, he made the statement pertaining to jealousy in the Spaniard: «It is indeed a received maxim in their country as well as in their theatre that love cannot exist without jealousy.» [6]

Violante attempts to put his mind at ease early in the play when she questions the logic of his misgivings:

...Sin que prosigas
más, di si es cordura o no,
que siendo tu esposa yo,
que tienes celos me digas.
(682-685)

Don Vicente's retort to his fiancée's question strongly indicates a natural tendency toward jealousy. In his

[6] ALPERN, p. 276.

reply Don Vicente implies that logically there is no foundation for his feelings, but he adds that Violante is responsible for the fault that is inherent in their relationship. The alleged fault is the one resulting from Violante's refusal to allow Don Vicente to make their betrothal public, causing the latter to consider himself «half husband» and «half lover»:

> no soy del todo marido,
> y soy del todo galán.
> Y así, divina Violante,
> no yerro en hablar celoso,
> pues he entrado a ser tu esposo
> sin salir de ser tu amante.
> (690-695)

What Don Vicente maintains, in essence, is that a lover is justified under any circumstances in being jealous of his beloved. One is forced to deduce that the protagonist, by his own admission, would have been jealous with or without provocation, thus substantiating the opinion of Hymen Alpern that the close association existing between love and *pundonor* is not the principal reason for having the recurring use of jealousy in the Spanish drama. Don Vicente's remarks to Violante lend credence to another statement made by Lord Holland about the Spaniard: «They seem to regard jealousy as sufficient to explain any absurdity and warrant any outrage.» [7]

Shortly thereafter, Don Vicente echoes this sentiment of justifiable jealousy when Violante hurriedly orders Leonor to blow out the light for fear of being discovered by her father who calls to her from within. Don Vicente states his conviction in these words:

---

[7] ALPERN, p. 278 .

...Agora,
pues te turban tus rigores,
no será justo que ignores
que tiene en tales desvelos
licencia de pedir celos
marido que da temores.
(706-711)

Although jealousy becomes a salient, identifying trait in the characterization of Don Vicente, there are other aspects to his personality that must not be overlooked. These diverse facets to his character are manifested in the manner in which he responds to personal attacks or tense situations. For example, when the young protagonist makes overtures to escort Violante from the villa, he is verbally attacked by Count Monforte for his intrusion. The Conde's intention to humiliate Don Vicente by brutally «putting him in his place» is received with admirable coolness on the part of Don Vicente. Rather than responding with caustic, biting words, the young man's rejoinder is calm and respectful. Don Vicente shows himself to be a man who can face adversity with serenity, capable of separating reason from emotion:

...que una cosa
es en nuestras competencias
ser enemigos, y otra
ser caballeros;
....
que nunca en los nobles llega
el disgusto a lo sagrado
del respeto y la belleza.
(329-338)

Realizing that Count Monforte regards him as an enemy, Don Vicente dispassionately points out the dichotomy between duty and personal feelings; for, even though bad blood exists between the House of Fox and that of Monforte, Don Vicente holds to the premise that respect for the individual and regard for beauty should not be desecrated by a gentleman in the interest of personal feuds.

Although Don Vicente gives the impression of being a man totally consumed by jealousy, driven only by passion, there are instances in which he proves to be quite rational. This sober side of his personality first emerges on the occasion of the King's initial visit to Violante. Don Vicente responds to the situation with mixed emotions. The torrent of words that he spues forth to his lackey at this moment of anxiety reveals his doubts and fears as well as a quality of self restraint. Witnessing the King's entry through the darkened balcony, Don Vicente is not certain of the man's identity. A sense of obligation compels him to intercept the intruder no matter who he may be. Checking his impulse, the protagonist addresses his lackey in words that disclose his innermost feelings:

> si me suspendo, sabrás
> que es porque he temido más
> mis desdichas que mi muerte.
> (753-755)

With this parlance Don Vicente satisfies an important drive, that is to say, he asserts his masculine pride. Even though he combats the compulsion to act against the night visitor, he makes his reasons clear to his servant (and to the audience). Personal dignity is preserved inviolate once he makes it known that he does not refrain from acting because he fears death, but rather because he fears more the repercussions that his unbridled behavior may bring about. In the end he refrains from an act that may satisfy his pride but may also put Violante's reputation in jeopardy. The incident reveals attributes heretofore undisclosed, that is, while Don Vicente has pride and valor, he also possesses prudence and a sense of responsibility.

Recalling the events that have tormented him in the past, the King's attention to Violante, Don Vicente's immediate reaction is to suspect the King of being the unidentified visitor:

> El Rey será ¡dolor fuerte!
> y así el temor de si es él
> me fuerza ¡pena cruel!
> y el ansia de saber yo
> la ocasión que ella le dio.
> Detrás de aqueste cancel
> escondidos nos pongamos;
> (756-762)

His effusion exposes qualities other than good judgment and cool thinking to be the responsible factors for Don Vicente's line of conduct. Overpowering curiosity mingled with jealousy influence his behavior. The overwhelming desire to learn whether or not it is the King himself who comes to visit Violante and, furthermore, to ascertain the degree of her culpability, force Don Vicente to take cover and wait. If jealousy has been the underlying emotion responsible for the conduct of Don Vicente, honor assumes a role of equal importance, for he utters to himself:

> ...Honor, suframos
> un instante; que no quiero,
> si infeliz me considero,
> creerlo sin mirarlo, pues
> aún lo dudaré después
> de haberlo visto primero.
> (766-711)

Although his preoccupation with honor is intense, Don Vicente exercises prudence and caution in waiting to witness for himself the evidence of Violante's guilt before he condemns her. He must see Violante's infidelity in order to believe it. So strong is his fear of disgrace that Don Vicente admits to himself that it will be difficult to believe that he has been a witness to his own dishonor. The fact that honor assumes an ever increasing importance in Don Vicente's mind becomes manifest by remarks such as the following: «Cielos, no se dé a partido / mi honor» (822-823).

In his role, Don Vicente embodies the ideals of the seventeenth-century gentleman in which honor dominates every aspect of his life. Once the protagonist establishes the King as a threat to his honor, he is guided in his every action by the code of honor that is a potent force in his life; by his mode of conduct, he shows himself to be very much a product of his time. For that reason Don Vicente confronts the intruding King with these words:

De secreto estoy casado
con Violante, y soy su esposo.
Pues me hizo el cielo dichoso,
no me hagáis vos desdichado.
Y perdonad, si osado
anduve; que más errara
si al ver mi afrenta, callara;
que desaires del honor
son muy terribles, señor,
para vistos cara a cara.
(832-841)

The phrase «no me hagáis vos desdichado» refers more to the disgrace than to the unhappiness that Don Vicente would suffer if the King were to continue his pursuit of Violante, knowing of her married status. What Don Vicente hopes to accomplish is to persuade the King to observe the code of honor. As a gentleman who suffers an affront to his self-esteem, Don Vicente must defend himself rather than remain silent in the face of menacing dishonor. It is for this same reason that Don Vicente shortly afterward is driven to enlist the help of Count Monforte in combating the King. Realizing that the Conde will rally to the cause of protecting his family name from scandal, Don Vicente points out to the old gentleman: «pues ya son / mi honor y el tuyo uno mismo» (956-957), and it is advisable, therefore, to put personal feelings aside and to join forces in saving each other from disaster.

In the characterization of Don Vicente, Calderón again shows his supreme understanding of human nature. It is made evident from time to time in the musings of Don Vicente as he ponders his imagined state of disgrace. For example, in Act III, upon his return from Mallorca, he plans to see Violante before making his official call on the King. Having sent Chocolate to announce his arrival, the protagonist remains behind only momentarily, just long enough to utter a remark that reveals his understanding of the workings of the human mind:

> A disimular, desdichas,
> vamos. Haced que no llegue,
> cielos, Violante a saber
> que en mí cupo la más leve
> desconfianza, porque
> propias y atentas mujeres,
> es decirlas que se atrevan
> el decirlas que las temen.
> (2641-2648)

From the foregoing passage it can be seen that Don Vicente realizes that he must use reason above emotion. He must proceed with subtlety and without permitting Violante the knowledge that he has doubted her fidelity, for to allow her this feeling of mistrust is tantamount to sanctioning her infidelity.

In spite of the fact that throughout the play Don Vicent is primarily driven by the mortifying emotion of jealousy, at crucial moments he displays other feelings that make him a very real and very human character. Wanting desperately to believe in Violante's innocence, he forces himself to give her opportunities to prove his suspicions to be ill-founded. If in the end he finds her guilty, it is largely due to the circumstantial evidence strongly against her.

From the analysis of Don Vicente's characterization it can be concluded that he is portrayed as a representative of the Baroque Age motivated by the baroque attitudes of his time. He acts much in accordance with the appraisal of Alexander William Herdler concerning the characters in the *comedias* of Calderón:

> The prevailing idea in Calderón's comedies is to exalt and exaggerate the sentiment of honor above all other sentiments; love, jealousy, valor, friendship appear in second rank and as if bound to enhance and give luster to the sentiment of honor. The father, the husband, the brother, the wife, the soldier, all entreat, threaten, fight and take revenge in order to redeem their honor, and they shun no sacrifice, no danger, and no crime in order to achieve that purpose. All the characters in Calderón's theatre conquer their desires, quiet their passions and sacrifice their dearest interests to obtain the reparation of an offence or the rehabilitation of their honor.[8]

Although greatly preoccupied with matters of reputation, there are, nevertheless, traits in Don Vicente that keep him from becoming a stereotyped, two-dimensional character. Despite his intense consciousness of honor, he

---

[8] «The Sentiment of Honor in Calderón's Theatre», *Modern Language Notes,* VIII (1893), 78.

still shows a capacity to restrain his emotions and to use discretion and good judgment when demanding situations arise. Being bound to the strict social ideologies of his time almost proves to be Don Vicente's downfall. Though he puts up a gallant fight with his inner feelings throughout most of the drama, in the end he very nearly causes the death of his beloved by allowing his imagination to dominate his reason.

In essence, Violante represents the woman of the seventeenth century. Possessing an acute and total awareness of her position in the society of her time, the heroine realizes that she may well become the propitious victim to be sacrificed in the act of restoring her husband's alleged lost honor. It is in this role that Violante falls prey to Don Vicente's vengeance despite diligent efforts to fend off all possibility of falling suspect to the sin of infidelity.

One can not help wondering if in selecting a name for his heroine, Calderón had in mind the word *violar*, symbolic of the presumed violation of her honor. The anxiety suffered by Don Vicente, after all, is based on this imagined violation of virtue. Since the heroine is never actually seduced — on the contrary she remains pure and faithful to her husband — the name of Violante ironically gains impact.

Violante's plight is threefold and a dilemma that prevails throughout the play, one predicament overshadowing another at different times. Half-way through Act I the heroine expresses her quandary in these words:

> Don Vicente, por los celos
> que de mí sin causa tiene,
> ha mil días que no viene
> a verme; de suerte ¡cielos!
> que hoy me hallo temerosa
> de mi padre, convencida

de mi amor, del Rey querida,
y de mi amante quejosa.
(557-564)

Thus, Violante must combat the overpowering emotions of three men: she loves Don Vicente; she finds herself fearful of the paternal wrath which results from this love; and she is forced at the same time to assuage the jealousy that engulfs Don Vicente as a result of the King's professed affection for her.

Among the qualities to be observed in the characterization of Violante are obedience, sincerity, goodness, and fidelity. Nevertheless, the one attribute which stands out above all others is her astuteness, especially with regard to understanding human nature. Evidence of this faculty can be seen in situations that call for quick thinking, employing common sense, or intelligently interpreting people's behavior.

In Act I, when Count Monforte discovers that both the King and Don Vicente are in his household, Violante realizes the futility of any attempt to explain the presence of the two men at such an unseasonable hour of the night. When asked by her father for an explanation of the circumstances, Violante shrewdly avoids the confrontation by answering the Conde's question with «Su Magestad lo dirá» (861).

In her conversation with Leonor the following morning, Violante shows intelligence in her understanding of human nature. Suspecting that her father has become aware of her relationship with Don Vicente, in spite of his having forbidden her to keep company with him, Violante is certain that the Conde's silence and mysterious actions are a prelude to the punishment that he is preparing for her. Relating to Leonor the unusual events that have taken place since Don Vicente and Count Monforte conferred in strict secrecy, the heroine logically, though erroneously, concludes that her condemnation and inevitable demise are near:

> ...Porque
> el que disimulos hace
> a su enojo, y no le riñe,
> es que trata de vengarse.
> (1306-1309)

Violante's shrewdness is again observed when Count Monforte returns from court bearing the good tidings of the King's permission for her marriage to Don Vicente. Anticipating punishment from her father, Violante attempts an explanation before the Conde is able to give her the joyous news. The old man, however, interrupts her attempted excuses, reassuring her that he has not come to talk about anything that she is imagining. Hearing from her father that he knows of her secret betrothal to Don Vicente, Violante erroneously concludes that the Conde is merely employing subterfuge in order to make her confess her true feelings for Don Vicente:

> ...(Él solicita
> con este engaño informarse
> de la verdad de mi amor,
> y le ha de salir en balde.)
> (1432-1435)

Astutely, Violante decides to beat her father at his own game. With her reply, calculated to throw Count Monforte off scent, Violante shocks the eavesdropping Don Vicente and confuses the Conde:

> A Don Vicente le diera
> menos la mano que a nadie,
> por no hacer en ningún tiempo

de las sospechas verdades;
y así, yo con Don Vicente
no casaré, aunque me mates.
(1438-1443)

Toward the end of Act III Violante sadly laments the unjust circumstances which have befallen her, attributing her misfortune to her ill star. With a keen sense of perception she enumerates the factors responsible for her ill luck, wisely concluding that the worst misfortune that can befall anyone is to be blamed for the blame that is not his. Now she discerningly ponders the gravity of her dilemma and wonders if she should return to her chambers, knowing that Don Vicente waits there intending to kill her:

Honor, ¿qué he de hacer? Si intento
volver a mi cuarto hoy,
dispuesta a mi muerte voy;
si temerosa me ausento,
añado otro fundamento.
Ir es desesperación;
no ir, confirmar traición.
(3113-3119)

In the face of adversity, Violante maintains a cool composure that enables her to evaluate intelligently her situation. Knowing the workings of human nature, she is aware that returning to her room now means the assurance of her own death; yet staying away means the confirmation of the guilt that is unjustly imputed to her.

Confessing the cause of her anxiety to Count Monforte, Violante reveals how completely she understands her dilemma. Her words show how totally aware she is of the futility in attempting to convince Don Vicente of her innocence:

¿Quién podrá satisfacer
cara a cara a un ofendido,
que contra sí mismo piensa
con razón o sin razón?
(3181-3184)

In the final analysis it must be deduced that Violante, being an innocent victim of a calumny, is worthy of compassion and understanding. Because she is a product of her society and because she must live by the mores of her time, she is virtually defenseless against the odds that threaten her life. Perhaps it is this circumstance that prevents the heroine from actively taking part in her own defense, and it is this circumstance that keeps her from emerging as a powerful character to be remembered in the same manner that the Queen will be remembered.

Imagery and Symbolism

Time and time again Calderón shows his remarkable deftness for brilliant and imaginative figurative language, avoiding the prosaic and stating the commonplace with poetic beauty. Throughout the play his images have been drawn from astronomy, mythology, nature, light and dark, and the animal world. From astronomy Calderón has taken the star to describe the beauty and majesty of the Queen Doña María. The star has also been employed as the force responsible for the ill fate of the Queen and Violante. Contrasting celestial images (sun-moon) and natural phenomena (light-dark, day-night) have been used to exteriorize the inner feelings of Don Pedro and Don Vicente. From mythology the author has taken the phoenix to sing the praises of the King. From nature he has taken the flowers to depict character. From the animal world he has employed the horse and the bull to personify the unchecked passions of Don Pedro.

A reference to the summer house opens Act I. In an effort to assuage the pain of unrequited love, the Queen is sleeping in the garden. A mood of serenity is conjured up by the description of the arbor which is apparently in the courtyard of the royal villa:

> ...porque en esta
> flórida estación, que el mayo
> fabricó a la primavera,
> ....
> se rindió al sueño en aquel
> cenador, cuya eminencia
> es verde cielo, a quien sirven
> rosas, y flores de estrellas.
> (2-12)

Spring and May are symbolic of flowers, images which are used to introduce the series of symbols that follow. The *flórida estación* refers to the summer house, and the tranquility of the atmosphere is emphasized by the *verde cielo* or verdor pervading the scene which is interrupted only by the flowers clustering about like stars. Symbolically carrying the theme of love is the rose which is the only flower specifically mentioned. The rose is traditionally regarded as the flower of love and beauty. [9]

Employed repeatedly, the star plays an important role in the imagery. The beauty of Doña María is compared by Violante to the majesty of a star: «...¡Qué su gran belleza / con la majestad no basten / a contrastar una estrella!» (46-48). Symbolic of fate and destiny, the star is also employed in exclamations of woe both by the Queen and by Violante. In Act I, Doña María replies to Violante:

---

[9] Richard FOLKARD, *Plant Lore, Legends, and Lyrics,* 2nd ed. (London: Sampson Low, Marston and Co., Ltd., 1892), p. 517.

Es tan ingrata mi estrella,
que aborrecida del Rey,
me quito de su presencia
(116-118)

Again, before the first act comes to an end, the Queen alludes to her ill star as the cause of her misfortune in lamenting her shabby treatment by the King:

casasteis conmigo pues,
y desde la hora primera
que en vuestra corte me visteis,
o fue rigor de mi estrella,
o fue envidia de mis dichas,
o de mis hados fuerza,
me aborrecisteis de suerte,
(259-265)

Later, in Act II while masquerading as Violante, the Queen attempts to convince the King that if it were within her power to make her feelings known to him he would discover that he is speaking to one who loves him dearly. Again Doña María alludes to the ill star as the force responsible for her misfortune: «pero su estrella ha impedido / el logro de tanta fe» (2042-2043). In his reply, Don Pedro, by contrast, shows his belief in self-determination rather than in the power of fate: «No hay estrella donde hay gusto» (2044). However Doña María reiterates her conviction:

Sí hay; que si la estrella es
árbitro de la fortuna,
y desde el azul dosel,
repitiendo los reflejos
con soberano poder,
a mí me hizo esclava vuestra,
y a vos os hizo mi Rey.
(2045-2051)

Thus, it can be seen that the Queen is convinced of the strong influence which fate has, not only on her destiny but also on the destiny of the King. Poetically she alludes to the sky that, as a blue canopy, holds the reflecting stars above. Destiny, the Queen continues, is what has kept her apart from the man she loves, and the gap existing between her and the King cannot be likened to the distance that lies between a flower and a carnation. The implication in this comparison is that since a carnation is in reality a flower, there is very little difference between the two; by contrast, the distance between Doña María and Don Pedro is immense. She states her case thus:

> Mi estrella es la que me aparta
> de vos; que no puede haber
> proporción en la distancia
> que hay de una flor a un clavel.
> (2052-2055)

Explaining the circumstances of the arrival of Don Pedro to the villa, Chocolate apologetically speaks to the Queen. The imagery employed in his speech is extremely functional in character depiction and plot development:

> Pero el caso fue, que andando
> a caza por estas selvas
> de Lates el Rey, siguiendo
> de un jabalí la fiereza,
> desbocándose el caballo,
> negó toda la obediencia
> a la ley del acicate
> y al consejo de la rienda.
> Desesperado se entró
> a la intrincada maleza
> de este monte, donde al valle
> despeñado...
> (145-156)

According to Juan E. Cirlot, the symbolic significance of the boar, as of most other animals, is ambivalent. On the one hand, it stands as a symbol of intrepidness and of the irrational urge toward suicide. On the other hand, it stands for licentiousness.[10] Thus, the wild boar hunted by the King represents the intrepid character and licentious nature of the King in his pursuit of an illicit love affair with Violante, a woman who is already betrothed to another man. At the same time, the boar symbolizes Don Pedro's irrational urge toward the spiritual suicide that will befall him as a consequence of his licentiousness. Supplementing the wild boar symbol is that of the horse. The two animals together convey powerful imagery that reinforces the playboy aspect of the King's personality. The runaway horse refusing to submit to obedience of rein and spur serves to emphasize further the monarch's intrepid nature and unbridled «animal» passion. Adding a final touch to Don Pedro's character is the headlong thrust of the runaway beast into the thicket and underbrush. *Despeñado* alludes to the riotous living which the King is wont to lead; the *intrincada maleza* (dense thicket and underbrush) again underscores his wild, «animal» nature.

Traditionally, in Baroque literature the fall from a horse symbolically foreshadowed the character's downfall. Since in this case the play ends happily, Don Pedro's fall from his mount only portends the downfall that he might have suffered had the play ended in tragedy.

Violante evokes beautiful imagery as she recounts the incident of her first meeting with Don Vicente:

---

[10] *A Dictionary of Symbols,* trans. Jack Sage (London: Routledge and Kegar Paul, Ltd., 1962), p. 29.

Una apacible mañana
de abril, a la feliz hora
que sale la blanca aurora
vestida de nieve y grana,
....
al campo sola salí
(623-630)

The white dawn symbolizes the birth of their love. In Violante's description, *vestida de nieve y grana,* the white snow represents her purity while the scarlet red stands for the fresh, red color of her lips and cheeks.

Don Vicente interjects: «Es verdad que yo te vi / en el campo entre las flores» (631-632). The allusion is very reminiscent of a love setting in the style of classic bucolic literature. In the ensuing lines of her romantic discourse, Violante uses other significant imagery:

Había por la ribera
vacadas, porque otro día
fiestas la ciudad hacía;
y una desmandada fiera,
a la querencia primera
volviendo, me dio cuidado.
Tú en mi defensa empeñado,
la resististe brioso,
tan valiente como airoso,
y tan diestro como osado,
por asegurar mi vida.
(633-643)

If it can be inferred that *vacadas* means both cows and bulls, the sexual implication may readily be perceived; the bull charging the maiden symbolizes the man seducing the woman. The attack on Violante by the *desmandada fiera* foreshadows the attack by the King on Violante's honor. Don Vicente valiantly runs to defend the maiden from the impending danger in the same manner that he later attempts to stave off dishonor by Don Pedro.

The device of the chiaroscuro recurs throughout the play with different images: day-night, sun-moon, and light-dark. The day-night combination is employed by Violante as she continues the anecdote of their dramatic meeting. She adds that Don Vicente and she became secretly betrothed after he conquered her aloofness:

a pesar del rubio coche,
de los hurtos de la noche
hiciese cómplice al día.
(669-671)

El rubio coche alludes to the moon which is regarded as the occult side of nature by its close association with the night. Night therefore represents the secrecy of the love which Don Vicente and Violante have vowed to each other. Calderón poetically conveys the thought that since the lovers are not able to declare their love openly in the light of day, day therefore is indirectly an accomplice to their secret in the same manner that the moon reflects light by robbing it from the sun.

Symbolically, light and darkness achieve a high degree of importance toward the end of Act I on the occasion of the night visit to Violante by Don Vicente. Hearing Count Monforte call from within, Violante orders her servant: «Leonora,/quita esas luces» (705-706). With the utterance of these words, darkness prevails from this point on—darkness representing misunderstanding, deception, secrecy, mistaken identities, and lack of communication. As the light goes out, Don Vicente is heard to exclaim: «Yo poco en las luces llego/a perder, pues estoy ciego» (713-714). The significance of this utterance lies in its symbolic meaning in that light is the manifestation of the intellect. What Don Vicente will suffer from now on is not physical blindness, but rather, blindness of the intellect. His inability to «see the light» by allowing his imagination to cloud his thinking almost brings tragedy to his life and to the life of the woman he loves.

The facility with which Calderón manipulates words may be witnessed in the short dialogue between Chocolate and Don Vicente following the discourse by the former on feminine flaws. Don Vicente comments on the triviality of his lackey's problems. The *gracioso's* rather intelligent retort illustrates the important role that the servant plays in his maser's love life. Chocolate speaks out:

> Señor, sí;
> que en esta amorosa feria,
> soy ganapán de tu amor,
> pues de Violante en la tienda,
> tú los conciertas y pagas,
> y yo se los llevo a cuestas.
> (439-444)

The word *ganapán* denotes a common laborer who, due to his rude skills, is capable of performing only work involving drudgery. Thus, in the reference to the *amorosa feria* (market of love), the lackey infers that Don Vicente's relationship with Violante may be compared to his dealings in the market place. That is, the master bargains for the merchandise (Violante's love) leaving Chocolate to bear the brunt of the burden (the complications of love) on his shoulders. Metaphorically, the servant vividly conveys the idea of the importance of his role in the love intrigues of Don Vicente.

Two striking metaphors are employed by Don Vicente as he confesses to Count Monforte that Violante and he are secretly betrothed. The first is used for the purpose of making the Conde aware of the serious repercussions which may result from the King's intervention in the love affair.

pues en un propio navío
corriendo tormenta están
juntos tu honor y el mío;
y no has de escapar el tuyo
del no esperado bajío
sin el mío, pues ya son
mi honor y el tuyo uno mismo.
(951-957)

Don Vicente vividly impresses the Conde with the reality that both are in the same boat and together they must weather the storm of menacing dishonor. Dishonor for one means dishonor for the other. Being keenly sensitive to the code of honor of his time, Count Monforte is willing to join forces with the man whom he formerly considered his enemy in order that his boat may survive the dark tempest of dishonor.

The second metaphor occurs when Count Monforte asks if Violante has given Don Pedro occasion for his nocturnal visit to the household. Don Vicente's reply is emphatic:

Si a oíllo,
ni a preguntallo llegara
de otro que de ti, imagino
que por las bocas del pecho
acabara de decirlo,
(971-975)

The implication of the question is considered to be so serious by Don Vicente that in his reply he insinuates that he would kill anyone other than the Count for making the same inquiry. His retort gains impact by the figure of speech which he employs, i.e., the offender would finish his question «through the mouths (stabs) of his chest.» The image painted in the mind of the spectator assumes an almost tactile quality.

Calderón's facile manipulation of words can be observed once again in the metaphor employed by Chocolate as he expresses his gratitude to Don Pedro for sparing his life after capturing him. The *gracioso* exclaims: «Seré de tan gran señor / escarpín eternamente» (2481-2482). Realizing that *escarpín* is the name given to a bedroom slipper or a soft shoe meant to be worn indoors, one can clearly perceive that what Chocolate is uttering is that he shall forever be at the King's feet, ever thankful for his generosity.

Day-night is contrasted again in Act II. Having received sanction of their betrothal even after Violante had erroneously led Don Vicente to believe that she did not wish to marry him, the lovers resolve their misunderstanding. As Don Vicente happily embraces his fiancée, he exclaims to her:

> Dame mil veces los brazos;
> que deseo asegurarme
> de que son míos, y dar
> al sol de mis dichas parte.
> Sepa el día mi ventura,
> pues ya la noche la sabe.
> (1522-1527)

Night, on the one hand, represents that aspect of nature which shrouds, obscures and fosters secrecy. Day, on the other hand, is the antithesis of night; all is made visibly clear and unobstructed by the light of day. In his desire to announce his good fortune to the sun, Don Vicente is poetically conveying his wish to make his happiness known to the world, for this happiness has been too long a secret.

Shortly thereafter, as Don Vicente prepares to read the letter sent to him by the King, he suspects foul play and blurts in an aside: «Cuidado, penas, que viene / envuelto en flores el áspid» (1574-1575). His remark is analogous to: «Beware the Greeks bearing gifts.» Don Vicente's suspicions prove to be well-founded, for although he receives an important title from Don Pedro, he is sent away on a military mission which absents him from his loved one. The asp has demonic implications and because of its viciousness, it is symbolic of evil.[11] Flowers, on the other hand, represent goodness and beauty. Although some good is contained in the King's message, the underlying motive is evil and conceived for the unwholesome purpose of seducing Violante.

Act III opens with a plaintive, short speech delivered by Don Pedro as he makes his way to the balcony where he hopes to meet Violante. Although the King is addressing Don Guillén, he almost seems to be delivering an aubade to Violante. In the highly lyrical passage Calderón exteriorizes the King's inner feelings, employing the baroque device of the chiaroscuro again.

> Pues la noche obscura y fría
> es a mi dulce querella
> más que el día hermosa y bella,
> más que nunca venga el día.
> (2142-2145)

In his joyful anticipation of seeing the object of his affection once more, Don Pedro first praises the beauty of the dark, cold night and in the same breath implores the dawn to come. The King's vacillating feelings are symbolized by the contrasting dark (night) and light (sun), for although the dark of the night is conducive to his sweet laments of love, daybreak represents the fulfillment of his yearnings when Violante will appear. In the mind of Don Pedro the images of Violante and the sun are fused as he utters the refrain:

---

[11] CIRLOT, p. 274.

y como la luna salga,
más que nunca salga el sol.
....
y como salga Violante,
más que nunca salga el sol.
(2150-2161)

One single allusion to light and dark, however, is not sufficient for the baroque style. True to tradition, the author chooses to decorate the King's speech with a profusion of light and dark imagery that may be likened to the heavy impasto of an artist's canvas. The device of the chiaroscuro is employed once more as Don Pedro sings the praises of the journeyman who sleeps without care, yet knows that he must rise at the break of dawn:

duerma una vez sin cuidado
quien tiene a que madrugar;
que menos no le han de echar
desde el lirio al girasol
las flores; que otro arrebol
es a ilustrallas bastante;
(2154-2159)

With great subtlety the transition from light to dark is accomplished, the sleeping man symbolizing night and the break of dawn symbolizing day. Adding a final touch to the light-dark imagery in the verses that follow is the allusion to the flowers; the whiteness of the lily representing the light as does the sunflower turning to follow the sun as it journeys across the sky.

Reference is made to some of the four elements in more than one instance.[12] Struggling to rid his mind of the tormenting doubts of Violante's fidelity, Don Vicente

[12] For an interesting interpretation of this subject see Edward M. WILSON, «The Four Elements in the Imagery of Calderón», *Modern Language Review,* XXXI (1936), 34-47.

utters self-deprecating statements in which he makes mention of the element of fire. More than once Don Vicente has seen the circumstantial evidence that points to Violante's guilt. Although he strongly resolves to withhold judgment of her, he cannot ward off the feeling of insecurity. In his anguished state of mind he cries out:

> En el mismo punto hallo
> a Don Guillén, porque aumente
> fuerzas a fuerzas la duda,
> visto el incendio dos veces.
>
> (2607-2610)

Possessing ambivalent symbolism, fire may represent eroticism, physical energy, or spiritual energy.[13] In the present context, however, fire is employed as an image of energy at the level of «animal» passion, that is to say, fire personifies not only the erotic «animal» passion but also the extreme jealousy which Don Vicente feels for Violante.

Allusion to fire and to air is made shortly thereafter as Don Vicente and Violante are united following their forced separation by the King. In his efforts to convince himself that his imagination has been playing tricks on him, and that Violante is indeed faithful, Don Vicente feigns composure as he greets her with these words:

> Tú seas, dueño mío,
> mil veces bien hallada,
> como has sido deseada
> deste preso albedrío,
> que en alas ha volado
> de amor, por llegar presto y abrasado.
>
> (2759-2764)

[13] CIRLOT, p. 101..

It should be noted in the foregoing passage that fire and air are mentioned only by innuendo *(abrasado* and *alas).* As before, fire employed as an image of energy, represents the physical passion felt by the lover as he makes a speedy return, on the wings of love, a figurative image alluding to air.

Toward the end of Act III allusion to light and dark is made again as Don Vicente and Don Pedro make their way to the balcony window where Doña María, masquerading as Violante, is to appear. Unaware of each other's presence, the two men approach the balcony, each preoccupied with his own thoughts, each motivated by different circumstances. Don Vicente in his depressed state of mind alludes to the night as a negative and unfavorable image:

> Ya que la noche ha bajado
> llena de sombras y horror ...
> (3223-3224)

Being in a happy frame of mind, the King alludes to the night, albeit indirectly, as a positive and joyful symbol:

> Ya que enamorado dél
> se va tras el día el sol ...
> (3225-3226)

Since the two characters are moved by different forces in their rendezvous, it is not surprising that the night image evokes both lugubrious and happy thoughts. In his disquieted mind, Don Vicente associates the night with sinister shadows and horror. Since the King's intention is to gain the favor of the woman he allegedly loves, his assessment of the night is favorable. He poetically refers to the phenomenon of night as the happy consequence of the enamored sun pursuing the day, the object of his affection. Repetition being a device peculiar to Baroque literature, these two contrasting attitudes are reiterated almost immediately afterward in passages that parallel the original statements. Don Vicente unhappily adds: «¿Habrá hombre más infeliz / en todo el mundo que yo?» (3231-3232). Don Pedro joyfully adds: «¿Habrá más dichoso hombre, / si logro aquesta ocasión?» (3233-3234). Again, the intention of each characer is stated once more in still another pair of verses as Don Vicente utters: «Hoy / mi honor tengo de vengar» (3240-3241), followed by the King's effusion: «Hoy lograré su favor» (3242).

In the final scene of the play when it appears that all will end in tragedy, Elvira arrives with a lantern. Symbolically at this precise moment, light assumes its most important role, for it is by this deed that everything is brought to light not only literally but also figuratively. As the light shines upon the characters they are physically illuminated as their mistaken identities are discovered; they are also spiritually illuminated as they realize their errors and forgive each other's human frailties. This is also the moment of climax, the moment when the pendulum swings from illusion to reality. Don Pedro, the antagonist, realizes that his pursuit was illusory because in reality he had been courting his own wife whose charms and merits he had unknowingly come to admire. Don Vicente, the protagonist, realizes that his grievance with his mate was, in the final analysis, based upon illusion and that Violante is indeed faithful. In the end, all of the characters come to the realization that pleasure and sorrow are ultimately based upon imagination.

Technique

The technique consistently employed by Calderón in *Gustos y disgustos son no más que imaginación* is the popular baroque element of appearance versus reality. Its importance rests on its pivotal function of welding the plot into a cohesive whole and in contributing most to the development of the theme.

Immediately at the beginning of Act I the Queen, upon awakening from her dream, sets the mood in which the technique of reality and illusion will be strongly in evidence throughout the drama. To Doña María, facing reality implies enduring the torment of unrequited love. Thus, being aware that her life is filled with pain and unhappiness, the Queen's subconscious employs a survival tactic that evokes an illusory happiness in her dreams. In the final analysis, therefore, Doña María experiences sadness in her waking hours (reality as it exists) and contentment while sleeping (illusion). She expresses her feelings to Violante thus:

Si soñaba una ventura,
y me hallo aora sin ella,
¡qué mucho, Violante hermosa,
que haber despertado sienta!
(75-78)

The technique is employed in other situations, involving other characters—Don Vicente's jealousy is exposed by the use of this tactic. To be sure, the latter's emotion is provoked before the play begins. (Violante and he later establish this fact in a long flashback.) The audience does witness the manifestation of his jealousy early in Act I when Violante innocently shows concern for the unconscious King. It has already been mentioned that Don Vicente's cryptic remark: «Qué piadosa estás, Violante» (177) later proves to be a strong indication of his jealousy. While Violante's attentions to Don Pedro are in reality an honest display of affection devoid of any romantic involvement, it is apparent to Don Vicente that her behavior signifies reciprocity to the King's fondness which is in fact romantic. Thus, the jealousy that will torment the protagonist throughout the drama is made evident by the technique of appearance versus reality.

Don Vicente's emotional disquiet is intensified near the end of Act I by the use of the same technique when the King makes his entrance through the open balcony, intending to force his attentions on Violante. Don Vicente's immediate reaction is to suspect that the unexpected visitor is there at Violante's invitation. Prejudiced by his deep-set feeling of jealousy, it is apparent to the young protagonist that his fiancée is in fact unfaithful. Overhearing their conversation and learning that Violante is equally as shocked at the presence of the uninvited Don Pedro, however, convinces Don Vicente that his suspicions are founded only on appearance and that Violante is in reality innocent of the guilt imputed to her.

In Act II the technique is employed as a vehicle for introducing deception as a theme. In his conversation with Don Guillén, the King presents himself as a truly contrite wrong-doer. From his words it is quite apparent to the onlooker that Don Pedro is truly repentant for being party to the disquiet of Count Monforte and Don Vicente, the cause being his unwelcome visit to Violante the previous night. In convincing verbiage he creates the illusion of being sincerely regretful of his ungentlemanly behavior:

> Mi dolor a esas causas corresponde,
> y entre tantos desvelos,
> con ser tanto mi amor, tantos mis celos,
> si de todo pudiera
> enmendar algo al lance, ...
>
> (1071-1075)

But with the departure of the Conde and Don Vicente, the King's true sentiments are made evident. The facade of repentance, regret, and remorse gives way to true feelings. Although he rationalizes his reasons to Don Guillén, Don Pedro has every intention of pursuing his courtship of Violante.

In the same act, Violante's fear of her father's wrath is based on appearance. Having left the King and Don Vicente to offer explanations to the Conde the night before, she is totally ignorant of the alliance which her fiancé has formed with her father. Violante's conclusions are therefore based on conjecture that is influenced by the Conde's mysterious behavior. The heroine interprets her father's unusual activity and silence as expressions of his brooding anger and as part of his scheming to punish her. Observing the apparent, she mistakes it for reality concluding that

> el que disimulos hace
> a su enojo, y no le riñe,
> es que trata de vengarse.
> (1307-1309)

Although blind to it, Violante in actuality is witnessing the arrangements for the sanctioning of her marriage. The delusion, nevertheless, does not end here. Suspecting her father of scheming to ensnare her into confessing her transgression in keeping company with Don Vicente, Violante herself resorts to trickery by denying her affection for her fiancé. The apparent truth of Violante's words has a twofold repercussion: the Conde momentarily doubts Don Vicente's sincerity; the latter feels duped by Violante. Thus the element of appearance versus reality once more functions as a vehicle of theme.

Don Pedro's gesture of generosity in bestowing the title of *maestre de campo* on his rival similarly rests on appearance. The King is motivated by less philanthropic principles than is apparent, for what the monarch essentially intends is to remove Don Vicente, the obstacle hindering his conquest of Violante. That the gesture is not really an act of good will is suspected by Don Vicente as he utters: «Cuidado, penas, que viene / envuelto en flores el áspid» (1574-1575).

At the end of Act II and during Act III when the Queen masquerades as Violante, the element of appearance versus reality is again employed. The device accomplishes two things simultaneously. First, Don Pedro, by accepting as real what is merely apparent, eventually comes to appreciate those qualities in his wife which he attributed to Violante. The King's conversion becomes evident when he utters to the Queen, although unaware of her true identity:

> Si hermosa os amé, Violante,
> discreta os adoraré;
> que esa hermosura del alma
> me rinde segunda vez.
> (2060-2063)

Second, Don Vicente's jealousy is rekindled as Don Pedro confesses to him (again, unaware of his identity) his winning of Violante's (the Queen in disguise) affection. Accepting as real what is only apparent, Don Vicente comes to suspect his wife of infidelity.

Finally, in Act III, appearance and reality as a device plays an important part in convincing Don Vicente of his supposed dishonor. Returning from Mallorca, the protagonist is willing to admit to himself that his volatile imagination is responsible for his spiritual disquiet. However, eavesdropping Violante's conversation with the King, Don Vicente is again fooled by appearances. Giving credence to the King's allusions to their secret rendezvous, while disbelieving Violante's denials of such meetings, Don Vicente is erroneously convinced of his dishonor. Both men fall into error, and their eyes will not be opened to reality until the climax of the play when the Queen reveals the truth to them.

Versification

In his use of metric forms, Calderón has not strictly adhered to the precepts set down by Lope in his *Arte nuevo de hacer comedias:*

> Acomode los versos con prudencia
> a los sujetos de que va hablando.
> Las décimas son buenas para quejas;
> el soneto está bien en los que aguardan,
> las relaciones piden los romances,
> aunque en octavas lucen por extremo.
> Son los tercetos para cosas graves,
> y para las de amor las redondillas.[14]

Instead, some of the verse forms assume other functions as the tempo and mood of the play change.

The *romance* is predominately employed throughout the play. Rather than being reserved for narration or to the *relación* (e.g., vv. 217-229, 236-298, the lengthy explanation by Doña María of the circumstances leading to her political marriage to Don Pedro), it is employed for several other purposes. First, it is used for conversations of varying moods: serious (e.g., vv. 882-1047, discussion of possible dishonor between Don Vicente and Count Monforte), emotion charged (e.g., vv. 2852-2872, accusations of infidelity made by Don Vicente to Violan-

[14] Félix Lope de Vega Carpio, *Obras escogidas,* ed. Federico Sainz de Robles (Madrid: M. Aguilar, 1946), II, 1447.

te), humorous (e.g., vv. 378-436, the discourse made by Chocolate on the flaws of women); second, for soliloquies (e.g., vv. 3061-3092, soliloquy by Don Vicente, planning to kill Violante and restore his honor); and third, for *quejas* (e.g., vv. 347-360, Vicente complains to Chocolate about the obstacles inhibiting the fulfillment of his love for Violante).

There are eight combinations of assonance in the play. Important to note is the fact that no one assonance is used exclusively for depicting one type of mood or emotion. That is to say, an assonance is employed in a variety of situations, be it serious or humorous, emotional or somber. In Act I, for example, the e-a assonance occurs in several scenes of sharply contrasting moods: in the beginning scene in which somberness prevails as Violante and Elvira discuss the Queen's unhappiness (vv. 34-58), Chocolate's comical repartee with Elvira (vv. 129-136), and the Queen's reproaches to the King which reach a high pitch of emotion (vv. 236-298).

The *romance* opens Act I and closes all three acts.

The *décima* (which assumes the form of the *espinela* in this play) according to Lope should be employed in complaints. Occurring in Act I (vv. 573-881) and in Act III (vv. 3093-3222), it nevertheless takes on additional functions in varied types of dialogue including *quejas, relaciones,* rapid conversation involving much action, conversation of an amorous nature, and short passages expressing great joy. In Act I the *décima,* used exclusively for Don Vicente's complaints of love to Violante, is sprinkled intermittently between verses 573-711.

The *redondilla* in its use for subjects of love, is more in keeping with Lope's suggestion than any other metric form employed. Its employment is linked to the love motif in Act I in the soliloquy by Leonor as she ruminates her dilemma to give assistance to the King in his courtship of Violante (vv. 449-496); again in the same act, Violante laments her misfortune in love by means of a short soliloquy (vv. 543-572). Ironically, the one instance in which the lilting motion of the *redondilla* does not function as vehicle for a love theme is when employed by Count Monforte expressing enmity and mistrust of don Vicente (vv. 497-542). In Act II the *redondilla* occurs once more in a long scene involving the love theme: plotting to continue his pursuit of Violante, the King gives a lengthy discourse on love (vv. 1180-1263). A series of scenes takes place later in the same act, all of which deal with the love topic: Elvira with a gossipy flavor to her conversation informs the Queen of Violante's sanctioned marriage to Don Vicente; Doña María, in turn, speaks of her unrequited love; Elvira advises the Queen to distract herself with music and joviality and thus alleviate the pain of rejection; Violante relates the favorable and unfavorable aspects of her recent union with Don Vicente; Count Monforte suspects the Queen of jealousy for Violante because of the King's affection for her; and finally Don Pedro expresses abhorrence for Doña María with the same enthusiasm that he expresses his love for Violante (vv. 1640-1863).

The *silva* is employed once only in the opening of Act II as the King speaks to Don Guillén of his supposed regret for the abrupt departure from Count Monforte's house the previous night (vv. 1048-1105), and in his conversation with the Conde regarding the marriage of Violante to Don Vicente (vv. 1106-1179).

The *sextina* is found only in Act III as Don Vicente greets Violante upon his return from Mallorca. This meter is characterized by the mounting emotional tension which pervades the atmosphere as the scene develops: the joy expressed by the lovers upon meeting (vv. 2747-2770), the tender concern displayed by Violante as she senses Don

Vicente's mental disquiet (vv. 2771-2782), Don Vicente's vacillating emotions of belief and disbelief in his wife's fidelity (vv. 2783-2793), Violante's emotional retort to his unconvincing explanations for his unusual behavior (vv. 2794-2806), the momentary allayment of Don Vicente's doubts (2807-2819), the tearful reconciliation of the couple as they embrace (vv. 2820-2829), and finally the abrupt interruption by Leonor, excitedly announcing the King's arrival (v. 2830).

TABLE I

DISTRIBUTION OF METRIC FORMS

Act	*Inclusive Lines*	*Metric Forms*	*Total Lines*
I	1-448	*romance* (e-a)	448
	449-572	*redondilla*	124
	573-881	*espinela*	309
		(Irregularity after line 646, and needed to complete *espinela)*	
	882-1047	*romance* (i-o)	166
II	1048-1179	*silva*	132
	1180-1263	*redondilla*	84
	1264-1639	*romance* (a-e)	376
	1640-1863	*redondilla*	224
	1864-2141	*romance* (é)	278
III	2142-2321	*espinela*	180
	2322-2648	*romance* (e-e)	327
		(Irregularity—line 2321 + missing)	

Act	*Inclusive Lines*	*Metric Forms*	*Total Lines*
III	2649-2746	*romance* (e-o)	98
	2747-2830	*sextina*	84
	2831-3092	*romance* (a-a)	262
	3093-3222	*espinela*	130
	3223-3366	*romance* (ó)	144
	3367-3370	*romancillo* (ó)	4
	3371-3396	*romance* (ó)	26
	3397-3400	*romancillo* (ó)	4
	3401-3426	*romance* (ó)	26
	3427-3430	*romancillo* (ó)	4

TABLE II

PROPORTIONS OF THE DIFFERENT METRIC FORMS

Metric Forms	*Lines*	*Per cent*
Romance	2151	62.71
Espinela	619	18.05
Redondilla	432	12.59
Silva	132	3.85
Sextina	84	2.45
Romancillo	12	.35
	3430	100.0

An Evaluation

In investigating what comment has been made by the major literary critics of Spanish literature regarding *Gustos y disgustos, f*ew critics have been found to consider the play worthy of individual mention among the works of Calderón. Menéndez y Pelayo stated that the play «está dentro de la esfera de la galantería más ideal» and with regard to the aspect of amorous intrigues which the play presents «no pasan de escenas de reja y terrero.» [15] Among the German critics, Schack had considerably more to say, heaping superlatives on the merits of the work:

> Este es uno de los trabajos más delicados y perfectos de Calderón, y que se distingue por su profundidad psicológica, por su análisis perspicaz del corazón humano, porque encadena nuestra atención, y por el enlace feliz que se observa entre su argumento y sus situaciones interesantes y bellas. La comparación de este drama con los datos históricos que le han servido de base, prueba el arte inimitable del poeta para dramatizar y pulimentar una anécdota descarnada é insignificante, no extenta tampoco de cierta repugnancia. [16]

Critiquing *Gustos y disgustos* almost a century later, Ángel Valbuena Briones also speaks of the play with very high regard. Among many other favorable comments he has this to say:

> *Gustos y disgustos son no más que imaginación* nos sorprende por su ágil y gracioso diálogo y por su ocurrente acción. Es una comedia que señala una vez más la riqueza de matices del dramaturgo madrileño. [17]

---

[15] *Obras de Lope de Vega,* ed. Marcelino Menéndez y Pelayo (Madrid: Sucesores de Rivadeneyra, 1898), VIII, cxlvi.

[16] Adolfo Federico Schack, *Historia de la literatura y del arte dramático en España* (Madrid, 1887), IV, 382-383.

[17] Pedro Calderón de la Barca, *Obras completas* (Madrid: Aguilar, 1960), II, 956.

Having just concluded an exhaustive analysis of the play, the results of which have been presented in the foregoing pages of this study, I am inclined to concur with the judgment of Schack that *Gustos y disgustos* is indeed one of the most delicate and perfect works of Calderón. Commentary and accompanying documentation have been presented in support of the thesis that architecturally the play is masterfully conceived; that is to say, the orderly subordination of the dramatic elements (plot, characterization, technique, and language) to a central theme (honor) makes of this play a superb example of baroque theatre.

Although the plot could be criticized from the standpoint of its inverisimilitude (the improbability of mistaken identities and the unlikelihood of the King mistaking his own wife for Violante without detecting the subterfuge upon hearing the Queen speak), it is no more improbable than other more celebrated baroque plays whose action revolves around the same device. *Don Gil de las calzas verdes* by Tirso de Molina, a play well known to students of Spanish literature and hailed as one of the best examples of Golden Age theatre, is held in such high esteem precisely for the technique of mistaken identities which complicate the plot strucure.

The effective use which Calderón has made of the baroque device of appearance versus reality not only provides more evidence in support of Calderón's remarkable craftsmanship in writing *Gustos y disgustos,* but also makes us wonder why the play should have fallen into obscurity. The evidence presented in this study upholds the belief that the device of reality versus illusion has been employed, if not with more success surely not with less success than in other Golden Age plays.

It is generally agreed that when Calderón reworked Lope's play, *El alcalde de Zalamea,* he succeeded in improving on it. The extraordinary vigor with which the characters were developed, Pedro Crespo in particular, and the dramatic intensity of the action, quite superior to the simple sketch by Lope, transformed the work into one of the true gems of Spanish literature. In like manner, the theme of *Gustos y disgustos* is based in part on another *comedia* of Lope. Here again, Calderón has achieved formidable success in improving on a character previously treated by Lope. One cannot deny, after reading both plays, that the characterization of Doña María in *Gustos y disgustos* stands head and shoulders above the characterization of the Queen in *La reina doña María,* written by Lope de Vega.

Notable in Calderón's literary production are his honor plays—plays in which honor and jealousy play important roles (e. g., *El médico de su honra* and *El mayor monstruo los celos).* Knowing that these plays rank among the most celebrated of Calderón's works, one wonders what factors were responsible for preventing *Gustos y disgustos* from achieving equal fame. This lack of renown could be attributed to a single factor, the fact that *Gustos y disgustos,* although it starts off as a tragedy, does not end in tragedy as do the other honor plays. There is no tragic end to Violante; there is a tragic end to the other heroines whose husbands are plagued by the same feeling of jealousy that plagues Violante's husband. While Violante does not ultimately die by the hand of Don Vicente, Doña Mencía (of *El médico de su honra)* is made to bleed to death at the orders of Don Gutierre who suspects her of infidelity. By the same token Mariene's death (in *El mayor monstruo los celos*) is ordered by the jealous Tetrarch of Jerusalem, out of dread that she should be possessed by another after his death. It seems, therefore, quite possible that *Gustos y disgustos* loses impact due to its happy ending; had Violante become a tragic victim of circumstance, the emotional impact of the drama would have been preserved, thus making the play more memorable to audiences.

In conclusion, it should be noted in concurrence with Schack's judgment that chief among the play's most distinguishing features is the penetrating psychological depiction of the characters which shows a profound understanding of human nature on the part of the author.

CHAPTER V

METHOD AND PROCEDURE

The compilation of the present edition of *Gustos y disgustos son no más que imaginación* is based on the first known printed edition in the collection *Comedias nuevas escogidas de los mejores ingenios de España. Octava parte,* 1657. Inasmuch as no original manuscript is known to exist, it seems logical to assume that the 1657 edition most accurately reproduces the *comedia* as Calderón wrote it. However, taking into account the poor editing and the careless omissions made by the printer, verses which were deemed to have been included in the original text were restored by relying on the emendations found in the Vera Tassis edition (1694), on the assumption that Vera Tassis who styled himself «el mayor amigo» of Calderón made the corrections from sources not accessible to others. These emendations are noted in the list of variants. It must be emphasized, nevertheless, that no emendations made by Vera Tassis have been accepted without first investigating their merit. In many cases the intervention of Vera Tassis on the works of Calderón is beneficial in making the meaning of a passage more clear. His value as an editor is demonstrated in the following example: In the first part of Act I, the metric form employed is the *romance* in e-a. When the Queen asks: «¿Quién está aquí?» (verse 65), Violante's response: «Quien humilde / a tus pies, tus manos besa» ends in the e-a assonance (verses 65-66). In the 1657 edition, the Queen's utterance: «Violante, estés norabuena» (verse 68), also ends in the e-a assonance, indicating that a verse is missing. The Vera Tassis edition corrects for the inconsistency in the metric form by supplying Elvira's interjection: «Es Violante de Cardona» (verse 67). Notwithstanding, in some instances it happens that in supplying corrections, Vera Tassis makes mistakes of his own. Of more serious nature are the arbitrary changes made which are not called for by the textual requirements. Examples of these arbitrary alterations are taken from Act I. In verse 197 where the metric form employed consists of eight syllables in *romance,* Vera Tassis changes the word order of *ningún riesgo* to *riesgo ninguno,* adding an extra syllable to the octosyllabic meter. In verse 612 he arbitrarily attaches the pronoun *la* to *hablar (hablarla)* and in so doing disrupts the eight syllable metric form of the *espinela.* Changes brought about by illogical intervention such as those cited above have been disregarded in compiling the present edition.

Since most of the important editions of Calderón's works published after 1700 derive directly or indirectly from the Vera Tassis edition, no other editions have been collated with the *princeps* edition of 1657. Printing errors of both editions were noted in the list of variants with the exception of words with obvious transposition of letters that could not possibly alter the meaning of the passage. Words with orthographic differences peculiar to the seventeenth century such as *vozes-voces* were omitted from the list of variants.

With an aim to present a more appealing and readable text to the modern scholar, the spelling, punctuation, and capitalization have been modernized. However, in order to preserve the meter of the verse, the following archaic forms have been retained: *aqueste* (and variations *aquesta, aquesto), priesa,* the paragogic *e* in *felize* and *infelize,* and *habemos.* In addition, certain words of the *princeps* edition have been reproduced for the sole reason of retaining the spirit of the seventeenth-century publication and to lend to the whimsy of the baroque language. Examples of these forms are the contractions *desta, della, dellos* and *dél;* the assimilation of infinitive+pronoun *(albergalle, oíllo, preguntallo, besalle, guardalle,* and *ilustrallos);* words which are known particularly for their vacillating orthography in the seventeenth century *(aora, agora, mesma, trujo, escuras, ansí);* words characteristically omitting the *c* or the *p* from the consonant clusters *ct* and *pt (efeto, vitoria, efetuado,* and *acete).* The spelling of titles with a capital letter has been made uniform throughout the text *(Don, Doña, Rey,* and *Reina).* Stage directions are taken primarily from the *princeps* edition but corrections are made in most cases from the Vera Tassis edition.

Although no arbitrary changes of words or phrases have been made for aesthetic reasons, a few changes in the spelling of words were made for the sake of improving the clarity of the passage. In situations in which the Vera Tassis edition differed from the 1657 edition in a word or phrase, preference was always given to the text of the *princeps* edition except where the Vera Tassis edition made more sense. The careless omissions in the *princeps* edition were always rectified from the Vera

Tassis edition and recorded in the collation of variants listed in a section following the text.

In an effort to present a clean, readable text, free of clutter from mechanical trappings, all asides are enclosed in parentheses, precluding the use of the word *aparte.*

PART II

TEXT OF THE CRITICAL EDITION

LA GRAN COMEDIA DE GUSTOS Y DISGUSTOS SON NO MÁS QUE IMAGINACIÓN DE DON PEDRO CALDERÓN DE LA BARCA

Personas

El Rey Don Pedro
El Conde Monforte
Doña Violante, dama
Elvira, dama
La Reina Doña María
Leonor, dueña
Don Guillén
Don Vicente
Chocolate, gracioso

JORNADA PRIMERA

Salen por una puerta el Conde y Violante su hija y acompañamiento, y por otra Doña Elvira.

Elvira. Tened, no paséis de aquí,
señor Conde, porque en esta
flórida estación, que el mayo
fabricó a la primavera,
andando aora con las damas 5

la magestad de la Reina,
mi señora, divirtiendo
la pasión de su tristeza,
se rindió al sueño en aquel
cenador, cuya eminencia 10
es verde cielo, a quien sirven
rosas y flores de estrellas.
Sola yo, que soy de guarda,
me he quedado; y así, es fuerza
que yo, señor, os dé el orden, 15
y que con él os detenga.

CONDE. Cuando yo, Elvira divina,
que es paraíso no viera
esta estancia, la juzgara,
con tal ángel a sus puertas. 20
Acompañando a Violante,
mi hija, que humilde espera
en este hermoso retiro
besar la mano a su Alteza,
entré hasta aquí; pero ya 25
que con vos, señora, queda,
me iré, envidiando sus dichas.
Caballeros, vamos fuera. *(Vanse.)*

VIOLANTE. Dame, bellísima Elvira,
los brazos.

ELVIRA. Y el alma, en muestras 30
de amistad.

VIOLANTE. No hagas ya
obligación lo que es deuda.
¿Cómo está su Magestad,
después que a aliviar sus penas,

dejando la corte, vino 35
a Miravalle, esta amena
quinta, que a orillas del Hebro
es doctísima academia,
donde sus primores ve
sabia la naturaleza? 40

ELVIRA. Su grande melancolía
en la soledad no cesa.

VIOLANTE. No me espanto de que así
llore, Elvira, y se entristezca,
mirándose aborrecida 45
del Rey. ¡Qué su gran belleza
con la magestad no basten
a contrastar una estrella!
Mas la condición del Rey
es terrible. Todos cuentan 50
crueldades suyas. Parece
que el nombre de Pedro lleva
estas desdichas tras sí,
pues tres Pedros ...

ELVIRA. Tente, espera,
y habla, Violante, más quedo; 55
que habemos llegado cerca
de adonde duerme.

VIOLANTE. ¡Qué hermosa
está dormida e inquieta!

(Como entre sueños.)

REINA. Mi Rey, mi señor, mi esposo,
haga esta felice prenda 60
paces entre ... Mas ¡ay triste!

¡Qué vana es y qué ligera (*Despierta.*)
la dicha del desdichado,
pues sólo el sueño la engendra!
¿Quién está aquí?

VIOLANTE. Quien humilde 65
a tus pies, tus manos besa.

ELVIRA. Es Violante de Cardona.

REINA. Violante, estés norabuena.

VIOLANTE. De tus tristezas, señora,
preguntaba a Elvira bella 70
el estado, cuando el sueño
tuyo me dio la respuesta,
pues que tan sobresaltada,
y dando voces despiertas.

REINA. Si soñaba una ventura, 75
y me hallo aora sin ella,
¡qué mucho, Violante hermosa,
que haber despertado sienta!

VIOLANTE. Ya que le debes al sueño
esa lisonja pequeña, 80
dilátala con contarla,
porque un rato la diviertas.

REINA. Soñaba, amigas; ¿quién duda
que soñaba, puesto que era
tan gran dicha como hallarme 85
del Rey adorada? Desta
novedad, tan novedad,
que no espero que acontezca,
era el medianero un hijo

que Dios me daba, de prendas 90
tan generosas, de tantas
virtudes, tantas grandezas,
que ceñido de laureles
en las moríficas fronteras
de Aragón, restituía 95
a su corona a Valencia;
tanto, que le apellidaba,
lleno de plumas y lenguas,
Don Jaime el Conquistador,
la fama por excelencia. 100
Este imaginado parto
mudaba al Rey de manera,
que enamorado de mí,
trocaba sus asperezas
en amorosos alhagos. 105
Dichosa, alegre y contenta
estaba, cuando del sueño
desperté. Mirad si es fuerza
que llore haber despertado,
pues veo por experiencia 110
que me hallé alegre dormida,
y me hallo triste despierta.

VIOLANTE. El cielo te cumplirá
el sueño, para que tengas
el contento sucedido. 115

REINA. Es tan ingrata mi estrella,
que aborrecida del Rey,
me quito de su presencia
en lugar de regocijo;
pues ¿cómo quieres que crea 120
en sueños?

(Hay ruido dentro.)

REY. ¡Jesús mil veces!

REINA. ¿Qué ruido, qué grita es ésta?

VIOLANTE. En este cercano bosque ...

(Dentro voces, y sale Chocolate.)

VICENTE. ¡Qué desdicha!

GUILLÉN. ¡Qué tragedia!

CHOCOLATE. Tal que, sea donde fuere, 125
he de entrarme por no verla.

ELVIRA. Hidalgo, ¿cómo hasta aquí
os entráis desta manera?

CHOCOLATE. Menos un perro que yo,
y más que esto es una iglesia, 130
y se entra en la iglesia el perro,
porque halla la puerta abierta.

ELVIRA. Salid de aquí.

CHOCOLATE. He de seguir
la metáfora, pues muestra
el *sal aquí,* que hemos sido 135
yo el perro y vos la perrera.

REINA. No os vais, deteneos, hidalgo.

CHOCOLATE. ¡Vive el cielo, que es la Reina,
como quien no dice nada!

REINA. ¿Qué voces han sido éstas? 140

CHOCOLATE. ¡O mi señora! ... si ya
acertará a hablar mi lengua;
que un tapaboca real
enmudecerá a una dueña ...
Pero el caso fue, que andando 145
a caza por estas selvas
de Lates el Rey, siguiendo
de un jabalí la fiereza,
desbocándose el caballo,
negó toda la obediencia 150
a la ley del acicate
y al consejo de la rienda.
Desesperado se entró
a la intrincada maleza
de este monte, donde al valle 155
despeñado ...

REINA. ¡Jesús! cesa,
villano, que ...

Salen Don Guillén, Don Vicente y el Conde; traen al Rey desmayado y siéntanle en una silla.

GUILLÉN. Entremos dentro,
pues quiso Dios que tan cerca
hubiese donde albergalle.

VICENTE. ¡Cuánto, señora, me pesa 160
de traer esta desgracia
a tus ojos! pues es fuerza
no excusarte del pesar,
porque algún remedio tenga.

CONDE. Por no haberme hallado aquí 165
la vida y el alma diera.

REINA. Mi Rey, mi señor, mi esposo,
¿qué desdicha ha sido ésta?
mas no merecía yo
dejar de veros sin ella, 170
porque el veros y no veros
sienta yo pena igual.

VIOLANTE. Deja
que den lugar los extremos,
para que se le prevenga
donde esté su Magestad. 175

REINA. En nada el dolor acierta.

VICENTE. Qué piadosa estás, Violante.

VIOLANTE. Piadosa no, sino cuerda.

REINA. Entra tú.

REY. ¡Válgame Dios!

VIOLANTE. Ya vuelve en sí.

REINA. Alma ¿qué esperas, 180
que no te das en albricias?

REY. ¿Dónde estoy?

REINA. Donde os desean
más vida que os deseáis;
gozeisla edades eternas.

REY. ¿Qué es lo que miro? No puede 185
haber sido dicha ésta,
puesto que he llegado adonde
lo que más me cansa vea.

VIOLANTE. Entre vuestra Majestad
adonde descansar pueda. 190

REY. Ya no puede ser desdicha
la mía, puesto que llega
donde tu crueldad, Violante,
de mi mal se compadezca.

REINA. ¿Cómo os sentís?

REY. ¿Yo? Tan bueno, 195
después que vi a vuestra Alteza,
que puedo, sin ningún riesgo,
dar a la corte la vuelta.
Don Guillén, dadme un caballo,
o el mismo, porque no entienda 200
que a mí me puede poner
temor ninguna soberbia.

REINA. Mire, vuestra Magestad,
cuánto en su salud arriesga,
y déme, como a su esclava, 205
para curarle licencia.

REY. Tengo que hacer en la corte.

VIOLANTE. Vuestra Magestad, advierta...

REY. No me he de quedar, Violante,
adonde tú no te quedas. 210

CONDE. Mire, gran señor, que ha sido
la caída de manera,
que peligra tu salud
en no hacer más caso della.

TODOS. Señor ...

REY. Todos me cansáis. 215
¿No sabéis ya cuánto es fuerza
no replicar?

REINA. Pues, señor,
ya que la ocasión desprecia
de asegurar su salud,
vuestra Magestad, atienda; 220
que no quiero despreciar,
virtud, o modestia sea,
es muy desaprovechada
virtud tal vez con modestia.
Cuando Aragón y Navarra 225
de duras lides sangrientas
aventuraban las dos
Coronas, fue conveniencia
del Conde de Mompeller,
mi padre ...

REY. Si acaso intenta 230
vuestra Magestad que escuche,
pues esta ocasión lo acuerda,
el que es hija de un vasallo ...

REINA. Por ser vasallo, ¿qué? ...

REY. Advierta
que en casa hablar de él y conmigo. 235

REINA. Yo cumpliré tan atenta
con los dos, que satisfaga
de hija y de esposa la deuda.
Vasallo mi padre fue;

pero de tanta nobleza, 240
de tanto honor, tanta fama,
tanto lustre, tantas fuerzas,
que si hubiera otro en el mundo
mejor que vos, cosa es cierta;
que con vos no me casara: 245
Mirad si es digna respuesta,
pues honro a padre y marido
con sola una razón mesma.
Y volviendo a mi discurso,
digo que fue conveniencia 250
del Conde de Mompeller,
mi padre, que en esta guerra
árbitro neutral, podría
dar la victoria a cualquiera,
que vos casaseis conmigo, 255
y que entonces su prudencia
aseguraría las paces.
Quísoos cumplir la promesa;
casasteis conmigo pues,
y desde la hora primera 260
que en vuestra corte me visteis,
o fue rigor de mi estrella,
o fue envidia de mis dichas,
o fue de mis hados fuerza,
me aborrecisteis de suerte, 265
que pienso que si hoy me viera
en ocasión donde hablaros
sin los decoros de Reina,
no conocierais; pues vos
me visteis con tanta priesa, 270
que percibir no pudisteis
las especies en la idea,
ni en el metal de mi voz,
ni de mi rostro en las señas.

Con esta desconfianza 275
viví, porque mi paciencia
presumía resistirlas,
ya, señor, que no vencerla.
Probando, ¡ay! ¡cuán en vano
con mis desdichas forceja 280
mi amor! pues cuando os escucha
un acaso que pudiera
hacernos de algún villano
huésped, porque la grandeza
de los acasos se mide 285
del hado en la contingencia,
aún no queréis serlo mío.
Ya del todo desespera
mi amor de que habrá ocasión
de que un agrado os merezca. 290
(Híncase de rodillas.)
Y así, señor, os suplico,
a estas reales plantas puesta,
que me deis para vivir
en un convento licencia.
Allí entre cuatro paredes 295
viviré alegre y contenta,
pidiendo, señor, al cielo
la salud y vida vuestra.

REY. A una Reina de Aragón
vendrále estrecha una celda. 300
Buen convento es Miravalle.
Guarde el cielo a vuestra Alteza.
Todos os quedad, y solo
Don Guillén conmigo venga.

GUILLÉN. Bien has dicho, porque tengo 305
de qué darte aviso, acerca

de que ya con la criada
está hecha la diligencia.

REY. (¡Ha, bellísima Violante,
qué de pesares me cuestas! 310
pero pues mi amor no basta,
yo me valdré de la fuerza.) *(Vanse.)*

Todos vuelven con la Reina.

REINA. Tampoco me acompañéis
a mí, que os tengo vergüenza,
testigos de mis desaires. 315
¡Denme los cielos paciencia!
(Vase con Elvira.)

VICENTE. Estarás con los extremos
del Rey muy vana y soberbia.

VIOLANTE. Quien no me ve cuando puede,
no me hable cuando se arriesga. 320

CONDE. Vamos a casa, Violante.

VIOLANTE. ¡Nunca esta tarde viniera
a ver a la Reina! pues
para mí ha sido tristeza
toda.

VICENTE. (Amor, disimulemos.) 325

CONDE. ¿Dónde vais desta manera
vos, Don Vicente?

VICENTE. Señor,
sirviéndoos, porque esto es deuda

de mi sangre; que una cosa
es en nuestras competencias 330
ser enemigos, y otra
ser caballeros; que fuera
muy grosera bizarría
que el enojo se entendiera
en la señora Violante; 335
que nunca en los nobles llega
el disgusto a lo sagrado
del respeto y la belleza.

CONDE. Decís bien; pero quedaos;
que aunque son bizarrías estas 340
hijas de vuestro valor,
tengo por opinión cuerda,
sin que puedan confundirse
en ningún tiempo las señas,
que el amigo y enemigo 345
lo sean, y lo parezcan.

(Vase con Violante.)

VICENTE. ¡Ay, Chocolate, qué en vano
solicitan mis finezas
vencer tantos imposibles
como a mis desdichas cercan! 350
El Rey a Violante adora.
La causa ¡ay Dios! es aquesta
por quien habrá tantos días
que hizo de su causa ausencia.
Y aunque es verdad que Violante 355
es mía, por tantas prendas
como tú sabes que hay
entre los dos, no me deja
declarar la enemistad
que ha habido en las casas nuestras. 360

CHOCOLATE. ¿Qué importa, si cada noche
que quieres estar con ella,
teniendo para este efecto
llave en traiciones maestra,
que de tu Rey y su padre, 365
uno ame y otro aborrezca?

VICENTE. Mucho, pues me agravia el uno
sin que el otro me consienta
poner reparo al agravio
con mi honor o con mi ausencia. 370

CHOCOLATE. En efeto, ¡no ha de haber
amor que, como en comedia,
lances de celos y honor
a cada paso no tenga!
¡Bien haya yo que en mi vida 375
quise bien!

VICENTE. ¿Qué tal confiesas?

CHOCOLATE. Sí; mas no es todo virtud.

VICENTE. Pues ¿qué será?

CHOCOLATE. Conveniencia,
porque cualquiera mujer
tiene mil impertinencias. 380
Si es hermosa, yo no puedo
sufrirla por su soberbia;
y ella no puede sufrirme
por la mía, si es fea.
Entre si es puerca o si es limpia, 385
hay la misma controversia;
pues si es limpia, tiene asco

de mí; della yo, si es puerca.
Y con si es discreta o boba,
en pie la duda se queda. 390
Señor, que si es boba, es boba;
y si es discreta, es discreta.
Y en efecto, en las mujeres,
que sepan, o que no sepan,
si piden, hacienda no hay 395
con que tenerlas contentas;
y si no, porque no pide,
para darle no hay hacienda.
Si da, ¡raro contingente!
que éstas son pocas y viejas, 400
con un lienzo piensa que
no regala, sino merca.
Si guarda fe, es perdurable.
No hay sino salirse afuera;
si no la guarda también, 405
que a nadie ofendido deja.
Si es doncella es un delito
en que no vale la Iglesia;
pues antes la Iglesia es
tribunal de su sentencia. 410
Si es casada y el marido
es duro, todo pendencia;
si es blando, todo regalo,
pues han de comer él y ella.
Si es viuda, a cualquiera riña, 415
del malogrado se acuerda.
Si es soltera, no es segura,
porque en efeto es soltera.
Si es mujer de obligaciones,
quiere que yo se las tenga; 420
y lo que hace por su gusto,
me lo pone a mí a la cuenta.

Si no es, a cualquier toma
me da un pesar; y es bajeza
que no valga más mi gusto 425
que lo que al otro le cuesta.
Sea en fin fea o hermosa,
puerca o limpia, aguda o necia,
pida o no pida, dé o tome,
fiel a mí o fácil ofenda, 430
sea en efeto casada,
soltera, viuda o doncella,
todas traen su inconveniente.
Y así, en las cartas primeras
de todas me voy, porque 435
no hay ninguna que me venga.

VICENTE. ¡Quién tuviera tus cuidados!

CHOCOLATE. ¡Quién los tuyos no tuviera!

VICENTE. ¿Tú los míos?

CHOCOLATE. Señor, sí;
que en esta amorosa feria, 440
soy ganapán de tu amor,
pues de Violante en la tienda,
tú los conciertas y pagas,
y yo se los llevo a cuestas.

VICENTE. Deja locuras, y vamos. 445

CHOCOLATE. ¿Adónde habemos de ir?

VICENTE. A verla,
que ya no tienen mis ansias
valor para tal ausencia. *(Vanse.)*

Sale Leonor, dueña.

LEONOR. Yo estoy en notable aprieto,
pues sola me vengo a ver 450
y un soliloquio he de hacer,
o he de decir un soneto.
¿Qué escogeré de los dos?
Al soliloquio me fío.
Aora bien, discurso mío, 455
solos estamos yo y vos:
hablemos claro. Mi ama,
tan constante como bella,
ama a Don Vicente; a ella
el Rey Don Pedro la ama. 460
Don Vicente es caballero
muy noble y muy principal;
pero tiene él mucho mal,
que tiene poco dinero.
Dos años ha que he velado 465
de balde las noches frías;
y el Rey en solos dos días,
dos mil escudos me ha dado.
Pues ¡aquí del discurrir!
¿No es mejor, quién lo dudó, 470
dormir y tomar, que no
no tomar y no dormir?
Uno vela y otro acuña;
¿pues quién es bien que prefiera?
Cuenta es ésta que la hiciera 475
cualquier zángano en la uña.
Y así, resuelta a medrar,
al Rey tengo de servir.
Este balcón he de abrir,
y aquesta cuerda he de atar, 480

(Abre un balcón y echa una cuerda a la parte de adentro.)

que es el orden que me dio
el que me trujo el dinero;
y pues que ha ya un siglo entero
que Don Vicente dejó
de ver a mi ama, movido 485
de recios celos, bien puedo
sin escrúpulos y sin miedo
hacer lo que me han pedido.
En falso cierro el balcón;
nadie lo puede advertir. 490
¡O, qué gran gusto es cumplir
uno con su obligación!
De luz y ruido se infiere
que ya mi ama llegó.
Esto es hecho; medre yo 495
y venga lo que viniere.

Salen Violante y el Conde.

CONDE. ¿De qué con tanta tristeza
vienes, Violante?

VIOLANTE. Señor,
pienso que el mortal rigor
con que hoy he visto a su Alteza, 500
de verla se me ha pegado;
que el sentir y el padecer
contagio debe de ser.

CONDE. Yo también vengo enfadado,
no de sus penas, aunque 505
las siento como es razón,
sino de la presumpción
y la vanidad, con que,
muy preciado de galante

cortesano muy prudente, 510
mi enemigo, Don Vicente
de Fox, se puso delante
de ti para acompañarte.
¡Vive Dios, que si no fuera
por ser en Palacio, hiciera 515
que aun ni a verte en esta parte
se atreviera!

VIOLANTE. Cortesías
fueron.

CONDE. Por eso lo digo;
que no ha de tener conmigo
mi enemigo bizarrías. 520
Mío su padre lo fue,
porque en la composición
de Navarra y Aragón
siempre mi opuesto le hallé;
y siendo así que él es quien 525
heredó rencor igual,
quiero, pues le quiero mal,
que no ande conmigo bien.

VIOLANTE. Bien pudiera responder
que no siempre ha de durar 530
la enemistad; perdonar
al contrario suele ser
la mayor vitoria; y más
cuando él rindiéndose viene,
y a servirte se previene. 535

CONDE. ¡Qué necia, Violante, estás!
y solamente te digo,
para que de aquí adelante

no le disculpes, Violante,
que sepas que es mi enemigo. 540
Éntrate en mi cuarto luego;
conmigo en él cenarás. *(Vase.)*

VIOLANTE. ¿Hay más desdichas, hay más
pesares que a tener llego?
No, que solamente en mí 545
tanto aunarse pudieron,
solamente en mí cupieron,
¡pues tan infeliz nací!
¿Qué Don Vicente, que ha sido
el que yo más he estimado, 550
es el que con tanto enfado
mi padre le ha aborrecido?
Y aún no para aquí el dolor
de mis sentimientos, pues
aún quedan otros después 555
que averiguar con amor.
Don Vicente, por los celos
que de mí sin causa tiene,
ha mil días que no viene
a verme; de suerte ¡cielos! 560
que hoy me hallo temerosa
de mi padre, convencida
de mi amor, del Rey querida,
y de mi amante quejosa.
Y si hubiera de decir 565
de todo lo que más siente
mi pecho, es, que Don Vicente
sin mí ha podido vivir
tanto tiempo. Leonor, di,
¿ha por ventura pasado, 570
siquiera sólo un criado
por aquesta calle?

Salen Don Vicente y Chocolate escuchando.

VICENTE. Sí,
que ya es justo responder
por ella; que aunque venía,
tan harta la pena mía 575
de sentir y padecer,
a darte quejas y hacer
alarde de su tormento,
ha sido tanto el contento
de escucharte de mí hablar, 580
que no ha dejado lugar
donde quepa el sentimiento.
Por esta calle he pasado
una y mil veces, Violante;
sólo he faltado el instante 585
que allá con el Rey he estado;
y esto no hubiera faltado,
a no verle mis desvelos
a mi lado; pues los cielos
saben que si allí vivía, 590
era porque allá tenía
conmigo todos mis celos.
Todos dije, y dije bien,
pues porque nada faltara,
hasta tu belleza rara 595
se apareció allá también.
No pude allí en el desdén
de mis desdichas hablar;
aquí vengo a descansar,
y tampoco puedo aquí. 600
¿Adónde pues, quieres, di,
que me vaya yo a quejar?

LEONOR. (¡Ay pena más inhumana!)

VIOLANTE. Leonor, a esta puerta espera.

LEONOR. (¡Ay Dios! ¡quién quitar pudiera 605
la cuerda de la ventana!)

VIOLANTE. Don Vicente, mi tirana
pena, mi fiero pesar,
muy otro se viene a hallar
hoy del tuyo; pues si a ti 610
te quita la voz, a mí
me da aliento para hablar.
No discurramos aquí;
calla tú, que yo hablaré,
y pues mía la acción fue 615
de poderte hablar así,
es justo dejarme a mí
hablar: a hablar me acomodo.
No extrañes estilo y modo;
que opuesto a nuestro sentir, 620
pues que todo lo has de oir,
tengo de decirlo todo.
Una apacible mañana
de abril, a la feliz hora
que sale la blanca aurora 625
vestida de nieve y grana,
a divertir la villana
pasión, que con mil rigores
todo era en mi pecho horrores,
al campo sola salí. 630

VICENTE. Es verdad, que yo te vi
en el campo entre las flores.

VIOLANTE. Había por la ribera
vacadas, porque otro día

fiestas la ciudad hacía; 635
y una desmandada fiera,
a la querencia primera
volviendo, me dio cuidado.
Tú en mi defensa empeñado,
la resististe brioso, 640
tan valiente como airoso,
y tan diestro como osado,
por asegurar mi vida.
Quedé, si no declarada,
desde luego enamorada. 645
Festejada y asistida
....
me vi de tus atenciones.
Mas ahorremos de razones,
pues lloran tantas bellezas,
cuantos consiguen finezas, 650
quizá por obligaciones.
Lo que embarazar podía
a mi ciega voluntad,
era aquesta enemistad
que entre nuestra sangre había. 655
Fue medio desde aquel día
que facilitó el favor;
porque como es rayo amor,
para mostrar su violencia,
en la mayor resistencia 660
hace el efeto mayor.
Correspondíte en efeto;
pero no ignoras ni ignoro
cuanto fui atenta al decoro
de mi honor y mi respeto. 665
Pues casada de secreto
me vi, antes que tu porfía,
venciendo la altivez mía,

a pesar del rubio coche,
de los hurtos de la noche 670
hiciese cómplice al día.
Desta manera, esperando
confusa nuestra pasión
de declararse ocasión,
gustosos vivíamos, cuando 675
el Rey me vio; y procurando
dar a entender sus desvelos,
sus ansias y sus recelos...

VICENTE. Esto diré yo mejor,
que si callé con amor, 680
no puedo callar con celos:
Viste al Rey...

VIOLANTE. Sin que prosigas
más, di si es cordura o no,
que siendo tu esposa yo,
que tienes celos me digas. 685

VICENTE. No lo es; pero tú me obligas
a estas culpas que en mí están.

VIOLANTE. ¿Yo?

VICENTE. Sí, porque si me dan
oculto el bien merecido,
no soy del todo marido, 690
y soy del todo galán.
Y así, divina Violante,
no yerro en hablar celoso,
pues he entrado a ser tu esposo
sin salir de ser tu amante. 695
Mi corazón, no te espante

si hoy como dama te ama;
que no se ofende tu fama;
pues entre amar y temer,
llegaste a ser mi mujer, 700
sin dejar de ser mi dama.
Luego... *(Dentro el Conde.)*

CONDE. Violante.

LEONOR. Señora,
mi señor llama.

VIOLANTE. ¡Ay de mí!

LEONOR. Ve, no salga.

VIOLANTE. Espera aquí.

LEONOR. Mejor es irte.

VIOLANTE. Leonora, 705
quita esas luces.

VICENTE. Agora,
pues te turban tus rigores,
no será justo que ignores
que tiene en tales desvelos
licencia de pedir celos 710
marido que da temores.

(Vanse y llévanse las luces.)

CHOCOLATE. ¡Buenos y a escuras quedamos!

VICENTE. Yo poco en las luces llego
a perder, pues estoy ciego.

CHOCOLATE. Los dos pienso que lo estamos, 715
pues ni vemos ni miramos
del daño la contingencia
que trae tal correspondencia,
y es... *(Ruido en el balcón.)*

VICENTE. No hagas ruido.

CHOCOLATE. No he sido
yo.

VICENTE. ¿Luego otro hace este ruido? 720

CHOCOLATE. Concedo la consecuencia.

VICENTE. Ya es mayor mi confusión.

CHOCOLATE. Harto grande era la mía;
necesidad no tenía
de crecer.

VICENTE. ¡Fiera pasión! 725
¿No ves abrir el balcón?

CHOCOLATE. Sí, que como obscuro está,
y abrieron el balcón, ya
la luz se ve.

VICENTE. ¡Hado cruel!
Un hombre ¿no entra por él? 730

CHOCOLATE. Y grande.

VICENTE. ¿Qué espero ya?
sin que aquí... ¿Pero qué intento?
Callar y hablar es error.

Sale el Rey Don Pedro.

REY. No diga que tiene amor
quien no tiene atrevimiento. 735

VICENTE. Pero ¿tendré sufrimiento
para hallarme en semejante
ocasión, sin que constante
me atreva a morir?

CHOCOLATE. Detente.

REY. Todo a escuras y sin gente 740
está el cuarto de Violante.
Habré de esperar aquí
a que venga la criada,
pues de todo está avisada.

CHOCOLATE. No te despeñes así, 745
sin advertir que por ti
puede arriesgarse el honor
de Violante, y es rigor
no mirar...

VICENTE. ¡Fiero castigo!

CHOCOLATE. Que es casa de tu enemigo. 750

VICENTE. No detiene mi furor
esto; que tan triste suerte,
si me suspendo, sabrás
que es porque he temido más
mis desdichas que mi muerte. 755
El Rey será ¡dolor fuerte!
y así el temor de si es él
me fuerza ¡pena cruel!

y el ansia de saber yo
la ocasión que ella le dio. 760
Detrás de aqueste cancel
escondidos nos pongamos;
que aunque ella sabe que aquí
estoy, él no, y podrá así...

CHOCOLATE. Ya en escondernos tardamos, 765
que traen luz.

VICENTE. Honor, suframos
un instante; que no quiero,
si infeliz me considero,
creerlo sin mirarlo, pues
aún lo dudaré después 770
de haberlo visto primero.

Escóndense Don Vicente y Chocolate, y salen Leonor y Violante con luz.

REY. Ruido he sentido hacia allí;
pero de quien trae será
la luz, pues se acerca ya.

LEONOR. (¡O cuán infeliz nací, 775
pues para volver aquí
aún no me dieron lugar,
en que pudiese quitar
la cuerda!)

VIOLANTE. Deja, Leonora,
aquestas luces, y aora 780
vuelve allá dentro a avisar
si mi padre se levanta.

(Vase Leonor.)

REY. ¿Quién creerá que mi valor
tiene a una mujer temor?

VIOLANTE. Ya que ¡ay cielos!

REY. ¿Qué os espanta? 785

VIOLANTE. Señor, yo ...

REY. No os turbéis. Tanta
es, Violante, mi locura,
como fue vuestra hermosura;
della aborrecido, intento
saber si al atrevimiento 790
se le sigue la ventura.

VIOLANTE. ¡Cómo! ¿Vuestra Magestad
(¿Qué es aquesto? ¡Muerta estoy!)
ha venido aquí? ...

REY. Yo soy,
porque vuestra gran beldad 795
persuadió a mi voluntad
estos empeños, y no
volveré atrás, porque yo
soy a un tiempo Rey y amante.

VIOLANTE. (¿Quién vio empeño semejante? 800
¿Quién mayor desdicha vio?
Pues no sé si Don Vicente
lo oye; mas ¿qué desconfío,
si siempre mi honor es mío,
que esté presente o ausente?) 805
Vuestro amor, señor, no intente
con ciega resolución

profanar de mi opinión
la deidad que vive en mí;
pues sabe que no le di 810
ni aun la más leve ocasión.
Atienda de mi nobleza
al heredado respeto;
que soy quien soy en efeto
a los pies de vuestra Alteza 815
estoy.

REY. Con mayor belleza,
después que turbada os vi,
nada os defiende de mí;
que no importa.

VIOLANTE. ¡Ay de mi vida!

REY. Que así estéis más defendida, 820
si estáis más hermosa así.

VICENTE. (¡Cielos! no se dé a partido
mi honor!)

REY. ¿Quién podrá estorbar
mi ventura y tu pesar?

Sale Don Vicente.

VICENTE. El que fuere su marido; 825
que ya habiendo vos sabido
que lo soy, vuestro poder
no ha de quererme ofender;
que el amor es diferente
a una mujer solamente, 830
que a una mujer mi mujer.
De secreto estoy casado

con Violante, y soy su esposo.
Pues me hizo el cielo dichoso,
no me hagáis vos desdichado. 835
Y perdonadme, si osado
anduve; que más errara
si al ver mi afrenta, callara;
que desaires del honor
son muy terribles, señor, 840
para vistos cara a cara.

REY. No sé cómo mi valor
ha tenido sufrimiento
para tanto atrevimiento,
sin castigar mi furor, 845
tu osadía y tu rigor.

Saca el Rey la daga, se arrodillan los dos, y Violante le detiene.

VICENTE. A tus plantas estoy puesto.
Así estorbaré dispuesto
esa especie de crueldad.

REY. ¿Tú le guardas?

VIOLANTE. Es piedad. 850

VICENTE. Es ley.

REY. Es Amor.

Sale el Conde, y cúbrense los rostros.

CONDE. ¿Qué es esto?

VIOLANTE. Llenóse el número ¡cielos!
de mi mal.

VICENTE. (¡Qué infeliz fui!)

REY. (¡O! ¡quiera el amor que aquí
no me descubran mis celos!) 855

CONDE. ¡Dos hombres fueron, recelos,
adonde Violante está!

VIOLANTE. Pues estoy perdida, ya
descubrir es importante
al Rey.

CONDE. ¿Qué es esto, Violante? 860

VIOLANTE. Su Magestad lo dirá.

(Vase, y descúbrese el Rey.)

CONDE. ¿Vuestra Magestad, señor,
en mi casa y a esta hora,
rebozado? ¿Quién ignora
que corra riesgo mi honor? 865
¿Es éste de mi valor
el premio ¡ay Dios! que me da?
¿Es éste el lauro que está
para mis sienes dispuesto?
¿Qué es esto, señor, qué es esto? 870

REY. Don Vicente os lo dirá. *(Vase.)*

CONDE. ¿Don Vicente? ¡Otro castigo!
Pues cuando con justa ley,
voy de mi hija a mi Rey,
de mi Rey a mi enemigo. 875
Para escucharte me obligo,
pues el Rey la ley te da.
Di, ¿qué es esto?

CHOCOLATE. (¿Cuánto va,
según lo que hoy estoy viendo,
que se va mi amo, diciendo: 880
«Chocolate lo dirá?»)

VICENTE. Generoso Don Ramón,
Conde de Monforte invicto,
cuya memoria la fama
ha de negar al olvido, 885
Don Vicente soy de Fox,
si noble, lustre y antiguo,
tú lo sabrás, pues me das
el nombre de tu enemigo.
Si te he dicho mi nobleza, 890
no sin causa te la he dicho,
pues de un enemigo ha hecho
la fortuna en mil peligros
un amigo; de un villano
un noble no; y así fío 895
mi esperanza en mi nobleza,
pues lo difícil no pido,
sino lo fácil, supuesto
que ya que noble me hizo
mi fortuna, hacerme puede 900
de tu enemigo tu amigo.
La bellísima Violante
es, señor, a quien previno
el cielo por ...

CONDE. No prosigas;
que ya de verte, adivino, 905
apadrinado del Rey
en mi casa, que ha sido
el intento que a los dos
a estas horas ha traído

para concertar con ella 910
lo que no podréis conmigo.
Pues aunque lo mande el Rey,
y sea el tercero él mismo,
no te daré yo a Violante.

VICENTE. Ni yo, señor, te la pido, 915
porque en mi vida pedí
a ninguno lo que es mío,
porque es Violante mi esposa.

CONDE. Primero este acero limpio
en su pecho.

VICENTE. No tan presto 920
colérico y vengativo
te empeñes en la primera
pesadumbre que te digo;
que faltan muchas que oigas,
que nunca una sola vino. 925

CONDE. Pues dilas todas de veras,
que aun a todas no me rindo.

CHOCOLATE. Cosas de tanta importancia
se hablan mejor sin testigos. *(Vase.)*

VICENTE. Violante es mi esposa; el cielo 930
este casamiento hizo.
El suceso, el modo, agora
no apuremos sus designios.
De secreto desposados
dos años ha que vivimos, 935
siendo el silencio y la noche ...

CONDE. No sé cómo me reprimo.

VICENTE. Aún no es esto lo peor.
Guarda los templados bríos
para ocasión más forzosa; 940
pues cuanto hasta aquí has oído
toca sólo a las razones
de estado de tus designios,
que es nuestras enemistades;
pero no toca en lo vivo 945
de tu honor, que adoleciendo
está de mayor peligro.

CONDE. ¿Mi honor?

VICENTE. Tu honor y mi honor;
mira si hacerte es preciso
de parte ya de mis ansias, 950
pues en un propio navío
corriendo tormenta están
juntos hoy tu honor y el mío;
y no has de escapar el tuyo
del no esperado bajío 955
sin el mío, pues ya son
mi honor y el tuyo uno mismo.

CONDE. (Ya es de otra materia esto.
Adiós, rencores antiguos;
que con el honor no hay temas, 960
y él ha de ser preferido.)
Prosigue, no temas, di,
habla claro, pues ¿qué ha habido?

VICENTE. De Violante enamorado
el Rey ...

CONDE. (Pendiente de un hilo 965
el alma tengo.)

VICENTE. Escaló
el sacro homenaje antiguo
de tu casa, y por aqueste
balcón ...

CONDE. (No sé cómo vivo.)

VICENTE. Entró aquesta noche.

CONDE. ¿Dando 970
Violante ocasión?

VICENTE. Si a oíllo,
ni a preguntallo llegara
de otro que de ti, imagino
que por las bocas del pecho
acabara de decirlo, 975
porque quien pregunta, duda;
y de honor tan claro y limpio,
aun es la pregunta ofensa,
por ser de la duda indicio.

CONDE. (No me va desagradando 980
para yerno el enemigo.)

VICENTE. No le dio ocasión Violante;
él sin avisar se vino;
que como es rayo el poder,
hiere antes del aviso. 985
Estaba yo en esta cuadra,
mientras Violante contigo,
cuando por ese balcón
entrar rebozado miro
un hombre; reconocerle 990
quiero, y no me determino;

no tanto porque me hiciese
cobarde a mí mi delito,
cuanto por averiguar
si era llamado o venido. 995
Volvió Violante, y adonde
me dejó, en un proviso
halló al Rey que siempre amor
tales tropelias hizo.
Turbóse Violante, el Rey 1000
se disculpa, yo me animo
con el desengaño. Ella
confusa y turbada, él fino,
ella cobarde, yo triste
y él despechado, estuvimos, 1005
hasta que pensando ...

CONDE. Di.

VICENTE. Persuasiones de rendido
a fuerzas de poderoso,
a salir me determino
a embarazar con mi muerte 1010
mi muerte, diciendo altivo
que era mi esposa Violante.

CONDE. Fue bien hecho y fue bien dicho.

VICENTE. Al ruido ...

CONDE. No digas más;
todo lo sé desde el ruido, 1015
cuyo escándalo es forzoso
atajar en los principios,
porque no suene en la calle,
ya que en mi casa se hizo.

El modo para atajarlo 1020
es menester prevenirlo;
y solamente de plazo
de aquí a mañana te pido.
En la cámara del Rey,
y delante del Rey mismo, 1025
he de darte la respuesta.

VICENTE. Tanto de tu valor fío
que espero pondrás al daño
reparo, y no precipicio
que con ser mi obligación 1030
hoy, a todo trance mío,
poner en salvo a Violante,
no lo intento.

CONDE. Has discurrido
cuerdamente; que segura
queda ella, pues yo vivo. 1035

VICENTE. Eres prudente.

CONDE. Soy padre,
y ya el daño sucedido,
solicito el deshacerle,
no aumentarle solicito.
(Pues aunque sienta casarla 1040
con el que fue mi enemigo,
sintiera más ver mi honor
amancillado y perdido;
y en dos peligros forzosos,
cordura y prudencia ha sido 1045
con el peligro menor,
vencer el mayor peligro.)

JORNADA SEGUNDA

Salen el Rey y Don Guillén.

GUILLÉN. Pues te has levantado.

REY. Nunca más tarde despertó el cuidado;
que como es jornalero 1050
de tan grandes tareas, el primero
del mundo se levanta
para acudir a todos.

GUILLÉN. No me espanta
que el lance sucedido
desvelado, señor, te haya tenido. 1055
Yo, que en la calle estaba,
y que el paso y la calle te guardaba,
cuando vi que salías
por la puerta, y que en ella ruido hacías
sin recatarte nada, 1060
muerto quedé teniendo imaginada,
aun menos importante
pesadumbre en las iras de Violante.
Mira lo que sería
cuando oyó de tu voz la atención mía 1065
lo que te había pasado,
siendo empeño tan grande y tan pesado
como hallar de presente

en aquella ocasión a Don Vicente
y después dél al Conde. 1070

REY. Mi dolor a esas causas corresponde,
y entre tantos desvelos,
con ser tanto mi amor, tantos mis celos,
si de todo pudiera
enmendar algo al lance, sólo fuera 1075
el haberme ausentado
de allí sin que quedara efetuado
el casamiento y paz de Don Vicente
con el Conde; que fue muy imprudente
acción dejar allí dos enemigos 1080
sin terceros, ni medios, ni testigos,
tan ciegos, tan confusos, tan turbados,
y en un lance de amor tan empeñados.
Mas ¿quién, Don Guillén, fuera
tan cabal, tan atento, que tuviera 1085
en tales ocasiones
propias a lo mejor las atenciones?
Yo lo erré con ausentarme;
pueda hoy el conocerme disculparme.

GUILLÉN. Digno es de atención ese cuidado. 1090

REY. Muerto estoy por saber en qué ha parado
de los dos el empeño.

GUILLÉN. No ha sido tan pequeño
que pueda discurrirse
el fin; pero si debe prevenirse 1095
alguno, es que habrá andado
el Conde muy atento y reportado;
pues basta que se vea
introducida en él, para que sea

cuerda resolución la que tomase. 1100
Y porque a servirte evidencia pase
este discurso mío,

Salen Don Vicente y el Conde.

juntos vienen los dos, de que confío
que paz habrán ya hecho.

REY. El corazón no cabe ya en el pecho. 1105

VICENTE. Esperando en aquesta
sala, señor, estaba la respuesta
que anoche me ofrecisteis
dar delante del Rey.

CONDE. Muy bien hicisteis
en no verle la cara 1110
antes que yo contigo a hablar entrara,
que importa que convengas
en cuanto yo le diga.

VICENTE. Aunque prevengas
a sus ojos mi muerte,
en todo estoy dispuesto a obedecerte. 1115

CONDE. (¿Qué contra mi deseo,
mi venganza y mi cólera, me veo
determinado a hacerme
de parte de mis ansias, a ponerme
al lado de mi pena? 1120
Pero fuerza ha de ser, pues que lo ordena
mi honor así; que hacer es gran cordura
a violento dolor, violenta cura.)
A tus pies, gran señor, vengo rendido.

REY. (De nada me daré por entendido 1125
mientras no se declare.)

VICENTE. (¡Piedad, cielo,
en tanta confusión!)

REY. Alzad del suelo,
Conde; ¿qué pretendéis?

CONDE. Arrepentido
del tiempo que tus reinos he tenido
alterados, señor, con novedades 1130
que causaron las dos parcialidades
de la casa de Fox y de la mía,
paces con Don Vicente hice este día;
y para que se vea
que esta amistad eterna a los dos sea, 1135
sin que a borrarla nada sea bastante,
por fiador ha salido ...

REY. ¿Quién?

CONDE. Violante,
mi hija, que por esposa se la he dado.
Tu licencia me falta; y no he dudado
tenella, porque intento que es tan justo [1140
la trae anticipada. Y que es tu gusto
lo sé ya, y tú mismo me dijiste,
alguna vez que en confusión me viste,
sobre lo que en aquesto hacer debía,
que Don Vicente a mí me lo diría; 1145
y hallo, señor, que esto es conveniente
a lo que a mí me ha dicho Don Vicente.

REY. Está bien entendido;

muy cuerdo habéis andado y advertido.
Estimo, como es justo, la prudencia; 1150
y si no falta más de mi licencia,
ya la tenéis.

VICENTE. Dame a besar la mano,
pues hoy por ti tanto imposible gano,
como verme seguro
en las felicidades que procuro, 1155
siendo Violante quien las paces fía,
tu esclava, hija del Conde, y mujer mía.

REY. Bien dices, está bien, sea norabuena.
(¡Qué dé yo parabienes de mi pena!
mas reportaos, desvelos, 1160
no reventéis la mina de mis celos.)
Para gustos de amor aun luego es tarde;
no esperéis más.

CONDE. Tu vida el cielo guarde
la edad del fénix. Ésta
ha sido, Don Vicente, la respuesta 1165
que daros he ofrecido.
Vuestra es Violante.

VICENTE. A tus pies rendido,
señor, responda mudo
el corazón lo que explicar no pudo
la lengua; sólo os digo 1170
que un esclavo hacéis hoy de un enemigo,
aunque no es novedad la que yo alabo.
¿Qué enemigo rendido no es esclavo?

CONDE. No, no me agradezcáis hoy, Don Vicente,
la que no hice por vos; pues claramente [1175

se sabe que en el agrado que os muestro
nada os doy, pues todo era ya vuestro.

(Vanse.)

GUILLÉN. ¡Qué cuerdamente el Conde ha procedido!

REY. ¿Hanse ido?

GUILLÉN. Ya, gran señor, se han ido.

REY. Pues estoy solo contigo, 1180
y sin escrúpulo y miedo
de mis vanidades, puedo
hacerte, Guillén, testigo
de tan justo sentimiento;
salgan del pecho veloces 1185
poblando quejas y voces
la alta región del viento.

GUILLÉN. Pues, ¿qué novedad, señor,
aora a tales desvelos
te ocasiona?

REY. Amor y celos; 1190
y si fue bastante amor
a verme como me vi,
advierte lo que será
amor, que con celos ya
se conjura contra mí. 1195

GUILLÉN. Si tú mismo aora decías
que allí haber hecho quisieras
esta paz, y consideras
lo mismo que pretendías;
que no te queda, sospecho, 1200

que sentir nuevo rigor,
pues miras hecho, señor,
lo que quisiste haber hecho.

REY. De hacer algún bien, es tal
la alabanza, Don Guillén, 1205
que haciendo uno ajeno bien,
no siente su propio mal;
pues por consuelo se queda
lo bien que procede allí.
Luego en este caso, a mí, 1210
no hay elección mía que pueda
dejarme a mí satisfecho
de que yo lo hice, pues
ellos lo han hecho, y no es
consuelo el verlo ya hecho; 1215
y así postrado y rendido,
no hallo medio a mi dolor.

GUILLÉN. El olvido es el mejor.

REY. ¿Dónde se vende el olvido?
¿Ésa es cosa que la halla 1220
algún tesoro a comprar?

GUILLÉN. No, mas el quererla hallar.

REY. No digas tal, calla, calla;
que si olvido se pudiera
hallar, ¿quién no le buscara? 1225
Antes al revés, repara
en que no hay nadie que quiera
del olvido hallar la gloria,
que no se dé por vencido,
pues a comprar el olvido 1230
va cargado de memoria;

y yo, en fin, desesperado
de no hallarla, he de buscar
cuantos medios pueda hallar
mi desvelo y mi cuidado, 1235
para conseguir, Guillén,
de mi esperanza el empeño;
y uno que he pensado, creo
que es el que me está más bien.

GUILLÉN. ¿Querrás, señor, escuchar 1240
un consejo?

REY. Sí querré;
pero no le tomaré.

GUILLÉN. Pues no te le quiero dar;
que será segundo error
despreciarle.

REY. Y haces bien, 1245
porque imagino, Guillén,
que los gentiles a Amor,
Dios, y no Rey aclamaron,
siendo así, que los demás
Dioses, provincias verás 1250
que como Reyes mandaron.

GUILLÉN. Nuevo ha de ser el concepto.
Dile.

REY. Pues sabrás que fue
porque el amor no se ve
a otro parecer sujeto. 1255
Consejos por justa ley
tiene el Rey, pero Dios no.
Y así el Amor se llamó

siempre Dios, y nunca Rey,
dando a entender en bosquejos 1260
y sombra, que ha de tener
Amor, como Dios, poder,
y no, como Rey, consejos. *(Vanse.)*

Salen Violante y Leonor.

LEONOR. Si desta suerte, señora,
con los extremos que haces, 1265
das lugar a la pasión,
podrás resistirla tarde.

VIOLANTE. Si yo llegara, Leonor,
a oir consuelo semejante
de otra como yo, pudiera 1270
ser que llegara a estimarle.
Pero a ti, ¿cómo es posible
que te agradezca el que haces
de consolarme, sabiendo
yo, que tú la causa sabes? 1275

LEONOR. Que la sé es verdad; mas como
no he sido participante
della, lo quisiera ser
del consuelo.

VIOLANTE. Pues mal haces
en deshacer el dolor, 1280
si pretendes aliviarle;
que el consuelo de desdichas
es otra desdicha aparte,
que será a quien las padece,
persuadir que no son tales. 1285
Si sabes lo que hubo anoche
en esta casa; si sabes

que después que Don Vicente
solo quedó con mi padre,
después de varios discursos, 1290
que no pudo escuchar nadie,
mi padre le dejó ir,
y sin verme a mí ni hablarme,
en su cuarto se encerró;
si sabes, al fin, que sale 1295
de casa aquesta mañana
con aquel mismo semblante
que si no hubiera pasado
por él tan estrecho lance,
¿cómo dudas que habrá ido 1300
a buscar, para vengarse,
varios medios, y que yo
estoy en riesgo notable,
de su valor y mi muerte,
esperando por instantes 1305
la resolución? Porque
el que disimulos hace
a su enojo, y no le riñe,
es que trata de vengarse.

Sale Chocolate.

CHOCOLATE. Con más miedo que vergüenza, 1310
si bien no son novedades
no tener vergüenza yo,
y tener miedo, entro a hablarte.

VIOLANTE. Chocolate, ¿cómo así
entras? ¿no ves?...

CHOCOLATE. No te espante, 1315
que por la mañana pueda

entrar cualquier Chocolate
a visitar a una dama.

VIOLANTE. ¿A qué vienes aquí?

CHOCOLATE. A darte
un recado de mi amo, 1320
y a saber de ti.

VIOLANTE. ¿Y qué hace?

CHOCOLATE. Toda la noche se estuvo
clavado en estos umbrales,
serenísimo señor,
sin ser Príncipe, ni Infante, 1325
previniendo por si fuese
en tu socorro importante;
y hasta aora se estuviera,
si el sol, celoso o amante,
a cuchilladas de luces 1330
no le echara de la calle.
A casa se fue, y al punto
della salió; hacia qué parte
no sé, porque me mandó
que yo viniese a informarme 1335
de si había novedad
alguna en tu casa. Un paje
dijo que estaba en Palacio;
con esto me atreví a entrarme
hasta aquí, adonde aora 1340
lo has oído de mi lenguaje.
Di qué quieres que le diga,
y sea algo que aliviarle
pueda; que está el pobre joven
tan confuso, tan cobarde, 1345

tan desesperado, tan
postrado, y tan miserable,
tan aburrido, que temo ...

VIOLANTE. ¿Qué?

CHOCOLATE. Que ha de meterse fraile.
Y sea breve la respuesta; 1350
no venga el Conde y me halle,
que en gramáticas de amor
los sirvientes más leales
son personas que padecen,
sin ser personas que hacen. 1355

VIOLANTE. Di a Don Vicente que yo
estoy ... *(Dentro el Conde.)*

CONDE. Esperad, que antes
que vos entréis, solicito
hablarla yo.

LEONOR. De tu padre
es esta voz.

CHOCOLATE. No se dijo 1360
por ella la voz del ángel.

VIOLANTE. ¿Qué aun este pequeño azar
no ha querido perdonarme
mi fortuna?

Sale el Conde.

CHOCOLATE. Yo he de entrar.

CONDE. ¿Adónde?

CHOCOLATE. Adonde gustare 1365
vueseñoría, porque
soy tan cortés y galante,
que en mi vida entré si no
donde los Condes me manden.

CONDE. Parece que tenéis miedo. 1370

VIOLANTE. (¡Ay desdicha semejante!)

LEONOR. (Él le mata.)

CONDE. ¿Qué buscáis?

CHOCOLATE. Nada.

CONDE. ¿Quién sois vos?

CHOCOLATE. ¿Yo? Nadie.

CONDE. En tanto que me avéis dicho
todos estos disparates, 1375
he estado haciendo memoria
yo, de que os conozca antes
de aora.

CHOCOLATE. Pues no lo crea,
que hay mil memorias locales.

CONDE. De Don Vicente de Fox, 1380
¿no sois criado?

CHOCOLATE. ¿Hay tan grande
testimonio?

CONDE. Dellos eres.

CHOCOLATE. ¡Un Conde tan venerable,
de la moza de Pilatos
ha de aprender el lenguaje, 1385
y decir: *Tu ex illis es!*

CONDE. Aora bien, ya llega tarde
mi enojo; a todos comprenden
los perdones generales.
Idos con Dios.

CHOCOLATE. Ya estoy tal, 1390
señor, que en aqueste instante
aun con el diablo me fuera.

CONDE. Idos presto.

CHOCOLATE. Que me place. *(Vase.)*

VIOLANTE. Tantos disimulos ¡cielos!
¿en qué han de parar? 1395

CONDE. Violante,
¿estás sola?

VIOLANTE. Sola está
Leonor conmigo.

CONDE. Al instante
salte, Leonor, allá fuera.

LEONOR. (Aquí es el *requiescat in pace.)*

Vase, y sale Don Vicente al paño.

VICENTE. No me sufre el corazón 1400
dejar, desde aquesta parte

donde el Conde me ha dejado,
de ver qué dice o qué hace.

CONDE. Violante, yo he pretendido ...

VIOLANTE. Detente, señor; no pases, 1405
si es que has de darme la muerte,
con el discurso adelante,
sin conceder a mis ansias
tiempo para disculparme.
Sabe el cielo ...

CONDE. No prosigas 1410
en tus disculpas; que en balde
son ya, que para conmigo
llegan ociosas, y tarde.
Nada de lo que imaginas
es en lo que vengo a hablarte. 1415
Con mi gusto, ya lo es,
estás casada, Violante.

VIOLANTE. ¿Casada, y con gusto tuyo?

CONDE. Sí.

VIOLANTE. (Mis infelicidades,
¿qué esperan? pues no serán 1420
bodas que su gusto hace
con su enemigo.)

CONDE. ¿De qué
tan nuevos extremos haces?

VIOLANTE. Estoy pensando, señor,
que si esto es asegurarte 1425
de las sospechas que anoche

en ti introdujo aquel lance,
no haces bien; pues esto es
decirse, y no remediarse.

CONDE. ¿Y si fuese Don Vicente 1430
el que yo pretendo darte
por esposo?

VIOLANTE. (Él solicita
con este engaño informarse
de la verdad de mi amor,
y le ha de salir en balde.) 1435

VICENTE. (Aora es cuando le agradece
el que conmigo la case.)

VIOLANTE. A Don Vicente le diera
menos la mano que a nadie,
por no hacer en ningún tiempo 1440
de las sospechas verdades;
y así, yo con Don Vicente
no casaré, aunque me mates.

VICENTE. (¡Cielos! ¿qué es esto que escucho?)

CONDE. Cuando pensé que te echases 1445
a mis pies agradecida,
¡con estos extremos sales!
(¿Qué fuera que Don Vicente
a mí anoche me engañase
por librarse y conseguir 1450
con este medio mis paces?
Mal hice en hablar al Rey,
sin haber hablado antes
con Violante. ¡O cielos, cuántas
penas de una pena nacen! 1455

Mas yo lo erré, ya es forzoso
llevar el yerro adelante.)
Violante, que tus extremos
sean mentiras o verdades,
ya estás casada. Yo quise, 1460
primero que a verte entrase,
prevenirte de mi intento,
y decirte que mirases
la obligación en que hoy
te pongo; no pienso hablarte 1465
nada; y porque veas cuán poco
plazo el desengaño trae,
entrad, señor Don Vicente,
que ya os espera Violante.

Sale muy triste Don Vicente.

VIOLANTE. ¡Cielos! ¿es verdad? 1470

CONDE. Ni rehuses ni dilates,
Violante, lo que te mando.

VIOLANTE. (¿Hay cosa como rogarme,
lo mismo que yo deseo?)

VICENTE. (¿Hay cosa como mirarme 1475
yo en tantas dichas dudoso?)

CONDE. (¿Quién vio extremos semejantes?
¡Aora él triste, ella suspensa!
Mi honor de todo me saque.)
Violante, dale la mano. 1480

VIOLANTE. Basta que tú me lo mandes.

CONDE. Eres tú muy obediente.
Llegad; ¿de qué os turbáis?

VICENTE. Nacen
mis turbaciones de verme
dueño de dicha tan grande. 1485

CONDE. Pues no os turbéis; que aunque novio,
es para turbarnos tarde.
Ya estáis casados los dos,
y ya que en aquesta parte
yo mi obligación cumplí, 1490
venciendo dificultades,
cumpla cada uno las suyas;
después no se queje nadie. *(Vase.)*

VIOLANTE. Esta palabra te doy,
pues ya no hay de qué quejarme; 1495
que con una dicha sola,
que hoy la fortuna me trae,
en paz se ha puesto conmigo;
y aunque de tantos pesares
me fue deudora, con este 1500
bien le perdono el alcance.

VICENTE. Yo no daré esta palabra;
que aunque tantas dichas gane
como haberme declarado
dueño tuyo, bien tan grande 1505
me da con tanta pensión,
¡ay de mí! como mirarte
forzada para ser mía.
Hermosísima Violante,
¿hubo menester hacer 1510
tantos esfuerzos tu padre?

VIOLANTE. He visto tan pocas veces
a la fortuna el semblante,
que desconocí las señas,

y pensé que me engañase, 1515
por apurar la verdad
de mi amor.

VICENTE. Aquesto baste.
No digas más, que a quien
desea desengañarse,
a muchas penas sola una 1520
satisfacción es bastante.
Dame mil veces los brazos;
que deseo asegurarme
de que son míos, y dar
al sol de mis dichas parte. 1525
Sepa el día mi ventura,
pues ya la noche la sabe.

Salen Leonor y Chocolate, cada uno por su parte.

LEONOR. De lo que supe allá fuera...

CHOCOLATE. De lo que supe en la calle...

LEONOR. A darte mil parabienes... 1530

CHOCOLATE. Mil parabienes a darte...

LEONOR. Vengo.

CHOCOLATE. Yo también, y tengo
de hablar, dueña honrada, antes
que vos.

LEONOR. ¿Pues de cuándo acá,
lacayos parangón hacen 1535
con las dueñas?

CHOCOLATE. Yo no entiendo
parangónicos lenguajes;
sólo sé que los lacayos,
jurisdicción inviolable
tenemos sobre las dueñas. 1540

LEONOR. ¿Cómo?

CHOCOLATE. El argumento es fácil:
En la casa de un señor,
el lacayo menos grave
sobre el más grave animal
tiene dominio bastante. 1545
La dueña no es mujer ni hombre,
sino otro animal aparte;
luego mandará en las dueñas
quien manda en los animales.

LEONOR. Es sofístico argumento. 1550

VICENTE. Dejad los dos disparates,
y de mis dichas los dos
dadme parabienes.

VIOLANTE. Dadme
los parabienes a mí,
pues más feliz ...

Sale Don Guillén.

GUILLÉN. Perdonadme, 1555
si antes de pedir licencia
entro hasta aquí; que quien trae
buenas nuevas, por cortés
no es justo que las dilate.
El Rey, mi señor, haciendo 1560

de sí generoso alarde,
hoy quiere honrar a los dos.
De las mercedes que os hace,
los títulos traigo.

VICENTE. El cielo
mil siglos su vida guarde. 1565
Dos cartas vienen aquí,
y una para ti es, Violante.

VIOLANTE. Ábrela tú, porque della
quien es todo tenga parte.

(Lee Don Vicente.)

Doña Violante de Cardona: a
atento a los muchos servicios b
del Conde vuestro padre, c
os hago merced de la villa de d
Castellón, con título de Marquesa, e
para ayuda a vuestro dote. f

VIOLANTE. A su Magestad mil veces 1570
beso la mano, por tales
honras y mercedes como
a esta esclava suya hace.

VICENTE. (Cuidado, penas, que viene
envuelto en flores el áspid.) 1575
Ésta es para mí.

VIOLANTE. ¿Qué esperas?
con igual gusto la abre.

(Lee Don Vicente.)

Don Vicente de Fox: a mi a
servicio conviene, que hoy b
salgáis de Zaragoza con la gente c
que en ella está alistada, y vais d
la vuelta de Mallorca, donde con e
título de maestre de campo sirváis f
aquella campaña, y no os vengáis g
hasta que esté acabada. h

VICENTE. No es menor merced la mía.
(Dejadme penas, dejadme,
y lo que la voz no dice, 1580
haced que el cordel lo calle.)
Por una y otra merced,
Don Guillén, iré a besalle
la mano.

GUILLÉN. Quedad con Dios. *(Vase.)*

VICENTE. Él vuestra persona guarde. 1585

VIOLANTE. ¿Merced de ausencia recibes
con contentos semejantes?

VICENTE. Sí, que ausencia, dueño mío,
que más ilustre me hace,
es para hacerme más tuyo. 1590

VIOLANTE. ¿Y piensas irte?

VICENTE. Al instante.

VIOLANTE. Idos los dos allá fuera.

LEONOR. ¿Qué es aquesto, Chocolate?

CHOCOLATE. Allá lo murmuraremos. *(Vanse.)*

VICENTE. Pues, ¿qué quieres?

VIOLANTE. Preguntarte 1595
yo ...

VICENTE. Di.

VIOLANTE. ¿Dónde he de quedar?

VICENTE. En tu casa con tu padre.

VIOLANTE. ¿Sabes qué en ella hay?

VICENTE. Sí sé,
obligaciones y partes
tan ilustres ...

VIOLANTE. ¿No te acuerdas? 1600

VICENTE. No tengo de qué acordarme.

VIOLANTE. ¿No será bien ...?

VICENTE. No, señora.

VIOLANTE. ¡Respondes sin escucharme!

VICENTE. Sí, porque no se han de hacer
las menores novedades. 1605

VIOLANTE. La Reina me honra, y con ella ...

VICENTE. Tú haz lo que tú mandares;
que de mí no ha de salir
ningún medio.

VIOLANTE. Aquesto baste;
sólo licencia te pido 1610
para verla aquesta tarde.

VICENTE. Es muy justo que la des
de tu nuevo estado parte.

VIOLANTE. Si me quedare con ella,
mientras tu ausencia durare, 1615
¿disgustáraste?

VICENTE. ¿Por qué
de aquesto he de disgustarme?

VIOLANTE. ¿Agradeceráslo?

VICENTE. No,
pues por tu gusto lo haces.

VIOLANTE. ¡Anoche tantos temores, 1620
y hoy tantas seguridades!

VICENTE. Sí, que anoche amante era,
y hoy soy esposo y amante.

VIOLANTE. Pues adiós, que yo sé bien
lo que he de hacer.

VICENTE. Sí lo sabes. 1625
Pero mira, si dijeres
a la Reina que quedarte
quieres con ella en mi ausencia,
echa la culpa a tu padre,
diciendo que está de ti 1630
quejoso, porque obligarle
pudiste a que, a su disgusto,
con su enemigo te case.

Y no te acuerdes de mí
en esto, así Dios te guarde; 1635
que en esto sólo, mi bien,
te perdono el no acordarte.

VIOLANTE. Cuerdo eres. Adiós, Vicente.

VICENTE. Noble eres. Adiós, Violante.

Vanse, y salen la Reina y Elvira .

REINA. ¡Grande novedad ha sido! 1640
¿Quién, Elvira, lo ha contado?

ELVIRA. De mis padres un criado,
que a Miravalle ha venido.

REINA. ¿Y qué le pudo obligar
hoy al Conde Don Ramón, 1645
con tanta resolución
y tanta priesa, casar
su hija con su enemigo?
¿Lo que en tanto tiempo no
acabó el ruego, acabó 1650
el despecho?

ELVIRA. Sólo digo
lo que del criado escuché.
La causa ...

REINA. Di.

ELVIRA. No quisiera
que murmurar pareciera.

REINA. Prosigue.

ELVIRA. Dicen que fue 1655
haber el Conde sabido
que de secreto se amaban,
se escribían y se hablaban,
y sintiéndose ofendido,
con acuerdo y con prudencia, 1660
que es el ejemplo más justo,
hizo de la ofensa gusto
y del daño conveniencia.

REINA. ¡Dichosos ellos, Elvira,
si es que se quisieron bien, 1665
y desdichada de quien
aborrecida se mira
de su esposo!

ELVIRA. ¿No ha de haber
cosa que no venga a dar
luego al punto a tu pesar? 1670

REINA. ¿Cómo, Elvira, puede ser,
si es punto fijo a que van
todas las líneas derechas?

ELVIRA. Tus temores y sospechas
estos recelos te dan. 1675
Trata, pues, de divertir
tus sentimientos.

REINA. No fueran
sentimientos, si pudieran
divertirse.

ELVIRA. Yo oí decir
un día, señora, que era 1680

enfermedad el pesar.
¿Luego débese curar?

REINA. Di cómo.

ELVIRA. Desta manera:
No quedándote jamás
sola contigo, porque 1685
la soledad siempre fue
la que al triste aflige más.
Mil damas tienes, señora,
tan discretas como bellas.
Habla y conversa con ellas, 1690
pues tu mal ninguna ignora.
Ten música, haz algún juego
que te entretenga; y en fin,
baja, señora, al jardín,
academia del dios ciego, 1695
donde entre fuentes y flores,
divertirás tu dolor;
que es enfermedad de amor
que se cura oyendo amores.

REINA. Porque no parezca, Elvira, 1700
que en mí esta necia pasión
es ya desesperación,
aunque el pensarlo me admira,
me reduciré. Di a cuantas
me sirven que al jardín voy, 1705
y que bajen a él. *(Vase Elvira.)*

Sale con manto Violante.

VIOLANTE. Feliz soy,
pues he llegado a tus plantas,

puerto, esfera y centro en quien
descansa la suerte mía.

REINA. ¡O amiga! gana tenía 1710
de darte ya un parabién,
si es verdad lo que he escuchado.

VIOLANTE. Verdad mi ventura fue;
pero el parabién oiré
de un pesar acompañado. 1715

REINA. ¿Cómo?

VIOLANTE. Como a Don Vicente
el Rey a Mallorca envía,
y en el término de un día
le amo esposo y lloro ausente.
A darte de todo parte, 1720
como a mi Reina y señora,
vengo a Miravalle aora,
y aún tengo que suplicarte
una merced.

REINA. Pues comienza
a decirla, que ya está 1725
concedida.

VIOLANTE. Si me da
osadía la vergüenza,
lo diré: Habiendo sabido
mi padre que me servía
Don Vicente, y que vivía 1730
de mi amor favorecido,
aseguró su cuidado
de suerte, que hoy ha elegido
del Conde para marido,
y del Rey para soldado. 1735

Hoy se casa y hoy se ausenta.
Mi padre, aunque muestra gusto
de casamiento tan justo,
no es posible que no sienta
ver que le ha sido forzoso 1740
el hacer esta elección;
y yo quedo, en conclusión,
con mi padre, y sin mi esposo.
Y así, señora, quisiera,
por el temor que me da 1745
vivir con mi padre ya,
que tu Magestad me hiciera
merced de mandar que aquí
hoy contigo me quedase,
mientras de mi padre pase 1750
el desabrimiento.

REINA. A mí
me está, Violante, tan bien
el que me hagas compañía,
que por conveniencia mía
me doy a mí el parabién. 1755

VIOLANTE. Beso mil veces tu mano;
y pues mi padre ha venido
conmigo hasta aquí, te pido
por favor más soberano,
tú se lo mandes.

REINA. ¿Pues no? 1760
Dile que entre a este vergel.

VIOLANTE. Mira que no entienda él
que te lo he pedido yo.

Llega Violante a la puerta, y sale el Conde.

CONDE. Ya os habrá dicho, señora,
el nuevo estado que tiene 1765
Violante.

REINA. A mí me conviene
agradeceros aora
tan justa elección a vos,
tan cuerda y tan acertada,
como, en fin, interesada 1770
en las dichas de los dos;
si bien de aqueste contento
mucha parte ha deslucido
ver que tan presto ha seguido
al placer el sentimiento. 1775
A Violante la decía
que conmigo se quedara,
porque esta ausencia pasara
mejor en mi compañía.
Ella, sin vuestra licencia, 1780
no se determina; y pues
vivir con un triste es
de otro triste conveniencia.
Conmigo estará. Prudente
sois, Conde; y así no os digo 1785
más de que queda conmigo
hasta venir Don Vicente. *(Vanse.)*

CONDE. ¡Dichosa ella que ha podido
conocer tanto favor!
¡Y desdichado mi honor, 1790
pues a término ha venido,
que la Reina, sospechosa
del Rey y Violante bella,
quiera asegurarse della,
honrándola de celosa! 1795

Mas ¿no puede ser que sea
esto acaso y sin cuidado?
¡Qué propio es de un desdichado
que siempre contra sí crea!

Vase, y salen el Rey y Don Guillén con capas de noche.

REY. En esta parte el caballo 1800
oculto, Don Guillén, quede.
Porque si algo nos sucede,
sea fácil encontrallo;
que pues anochece ya,
más desconocido a pie 1805
a Violante esperaré
al paso.

GUILLÉN. Presto saldrá
de la visita, que no
querrá volverse más noche.

REY. Un hombre se acerca al coche, 1810
que de la quinta salió.

GUILLÉN. Y puesto en él, ha partido
a la corte sin Violante.

REY. En ocasión semejante,
¿qué podrá haber sucedido 1815
para que el coche sin ella
se vaya?

GUILLÉN. De algún criado
presto volveré informado
qué ha sido. *(Vase.)*

REY. ¡Ay, Violante bella!
¡cuán postrado a mi valor, 1820
cuán altivo tu desdén,
a un mismo tiempo se ven
batallando con mi amor!

Sale Don Guillén.

GUILLÉN. Preguntado a un escudero
cómo el coche se volvía 1825
sin Violante y sin el día
que había traído primero,
respondió, que se quedaba
a vivir ya desde aora
con la Reina mi señora, 1830
porque su Alteza gustaba
de que pasase con ella
la ausencia de su marido.
De que claro he conocido
que está de Violante bella 1835
la Reina celosa, o que
recatada y temerosa
de sí está Violante hermosa;
y de cualquiera que fue
la acción, todos tus desvelos 1840
vencidos, señor, se ven.
Si es Violante, con desdén;
y si es la Reina, con celos.

REY. ¿Habrá alguna acción que pueda
yo estimar a la fortuna? 1845
¿Habrá, Guillén, cosa alguna
que a mi gusto me suceda?
¿Quién en el mundo jamás
vio juntas, como yo agora,

la cosa que más adora, 1850
y la que aborrece más?
Llegue a su fin el tormento
de mi amor, llegue su fin,
pues ... ¿Mas qué oigo?

(Tocan dentro.)

GUILLÉN. En el jardín
ha tocado un instrumento 1855
Quizá su pena cruel
suele divertir así.

REY. Abierta, Guillén, allí
está una ventana dél,
por donde el aire veloz 1860
trae más distinto el acento.

GUILLÉN. Escucha, que al instrumento
acompaña alguna voz.

Cantan dentro, y a una ventana baja sale Violante.

MÚSICA. Arded, corazón, arded;
que yo no os puedo valer. 1865

VIOLANTE. Después que se despidió
de mí mi esposo, y después
que salió de Zaragoza,
ya despedido del Rey,
me envió desde el camino 1870
con Chocolate un papel,
diciéndome que al terrero
de la quinta vendría a ver
si en la quinta me quedaba

con la Reina; pues se ve 1875
con sus damas divertida
en la paz deste vergel,
quiero desde esta ventana
el sitio reconocer,
porque sepa que aquí estoy, 1880
si acaso viniese a él.

REY. A la ventana ha salido
una dama; llegaré
a hablarla, por si por dicha
alguna puedo tener. 1885

VIOLANTE. Un hombre hacia la ventana
se llega; sin duda es él;
pero no le quiero hablar
antes de reconocer
la voz.

REY. Puesto que no es culpa 1890
osadía tan cortés,
bien podrá un triste, señora,
que a aquestas horas se ve
a esta reja, preguntaros
si es amor la causa que 1895
os tiene tan desvelada,
por consolarme, con ver
que hay quien padezca en el mundo
las mismas desdichas que él.

VIOLANTE. (No es la voz de Don Vicente, 1900
ni conozco cuya es;
pero donde hay tantas damas,
es fuerza que haya de haber
galanes. Desengañarle

quiero, por quedar sin él.) 1905
Caballero rebozado,
que a estos umbrales os veis,
buscando de amor consuelo
que en amor no puede haber,
no soy yo la que esperáis; 1910
y así, idos con Dios.

REY. ¿Sabéis
a quién puedo esperar yo?

VIOLANTE. No; mas yo no puedo ser,
porque soy tan nueva aquí,
que ésta es la primera vez 1915
que he llegado a esta ventana;
y si en ella estar soléis,
no puede ser por mí hoy,
porque no estaba aquí ayer.

REY. Por las señas que me dais, 1920
me dais, señora, a entender
que sois vos la que yo busco;
que es la primer vez también
que llego aquí, y la primera,
si a mi dicha he de creer, 1925
que en la casa del pesar
está por guarda el placer.
¿No sois la hermosa Violante?

VIOLANTE. (Sin duda alguna criado es
o amigo de Don Vicente, 1930
que a disculparse por él
envía, por no venir,
quizá por más no poder;
que no supiera que había

de estar yo aquí, a no tener 1935
estas noticias dél mismo.)
Violante soy; ¿quién sois?

REY. Quien
es tan feliz, que buscando
un gusto, ha dado con él.

VIOLANTE. No es esto lo que os pregunto. 1940
Si el nombre no respondéis,
dejaré la reja.

REY. Soy,
pues que lo queréis saber,
dándoos por desentendida
de la más constante fe 1945
que el triunfo miro de amor,
él; mas luego os diré,
que viene gente, y es fuerza
retirarme hasta después.
No vean éstos que aquí estamos; 1950
demos la vuelta, Guillén.

Salen Don Vicente y Chocolate de camino por un lado, y el Rey y Don Guillén se retiran por otro.

VIOLANTE. El Rey es éste, que aora
le conocí. Dejaré
la ventana, y aunque venga
mi esposo, no le veré; 1955
que menos importará
el dejar de hablar con él,
que no hallarme en la ventana,
estando en la calle el Rey. *(Vase.)*

VICENTE. ¿No la diste el papel?

CHOCOLATE. Sí, 1960
y leyó todo el papel.

VICENTE. Luego ya avisada, es fuerza
que en alguna reja esté,
si en la quinta se quedó
con la Reina.

CHOCOLATE. No sé quien 1965
se vuelve desde el camino
a ver su propia mujer.

VICENTE. En ninguna reja hay gente.

CHOCOLATE. Pues parado aquí no estés,
que en hombres parados más 1970
se repara.

VICENTE. Dices bien,
y pues aquí no hacer señas
ni pararse puede ser,
demos la vuelta a la quinta.

CHOCOLATE. Dime, ¿suele suceder, 1975
de quintas en los terreros,
dar a alguno con algo?

VICENTE. Ven,
no preguntes disparates.

Vanse los dos, salen la Reina y Elvira a la misma ventana, y vuelven por otra parte o puerta el Rey y Don Guillén.

REINA. Ya que a este jardín bajé,
gozar quiero, Elvira hermosa, 1980
todas las delicias dél.
Di a las damas que a esta reja
gozando con más placer
el fresco estoy.

ELVIRA. A decirlo
voy, señora. *(Vase.)*

GUILLÉN. Ya se fue 1985
la gente.

REY. Alguien que pasaba
acaso debió de ser.
Retírate a aquella parte,
que todavía se ve
Violante a la reja, donde 1990
cuando me fui la dejé.

REINA. Un hombre llega a la reja.
la voz disimularé
para averiguar si acaso
alguna dama tal vez 1995
suele hablar, y no habrá sido
estar aquí en vano.

REY. Pues
no habéis dejado, señora,
la ventana, pensaré,
y no sin razón, que ha sido 2000
curiosidad de saber
quién soy, que es donde quedó
la conversación; si bien
se quejaron mis finezas

de que la noticia os dé 2005
la voz, pudiendo, Violante,
della saberlo más bien.
Mirad si queréis que os diga
más claro que soy el Rey.

REINA. (¡Válgame el cielo! ¿qué escucho? 2010
A mi fortuna cruel
sólo celos le faltaban
de sentir y padecer.
Ya está cabal el dolor.)

REY. ¿Quién, si yo no, fuera quien 2015
tuviera por centro tuyo
dondequiera que os halléis?

REINA. (De confusa, y de turbada
no le acierto a responder.
Pero pues de mi voz tiene 2020
tan poca noticia, haré
esfuerzos, disimulando,
para llegar a saber
el fondo de mis desdichas.)
Con poca razón se ve 2025
vuestra Magestad quejoso
de mí, señor, puesto que
corresponder a quien soy,
no ha sido olvidar quien es.

REY. Sí ha sido; pues en el día 2030
de hoy os llego a perder
dos veces, casada una,
y retirada después.

REINA. No me juzguéis tan ingrata,
tan esquiva y tan cruel; 2035

que no es ser cruel y esquiva
el ser noble una mujer.
Basta decir que si fuera
justo declararme, sé
que estás hablando, señor, 2040
con quien os quiere muy bien;
pero su estrella ha impedido
el logro de tanta fe.

REY. No hay estrella donde hay gusto.

REINA. Sí hay; que si la estrella es 2045
árbitro de la fortuna,
y desde el azul dosel,
repitiendo los reflejos
con soberano poder,
a mí me hizo esclava vuestra, 2050
y a vos os hizo mi Rey.
Mi estrella es la que me aparta
de vos; que no puede haber
proporción en la distancia
que hay de una flor a un clavel. 2055

REY. Sobre estos influjos tiene
el albedrío poder.

REINA. Para que los venza sí,
no para dejarse vencer.

REY. Si hermosa os amé, Violante, 2060
discreta os adoraré;
que esa hermosura del alma
me rinde segunda vez.

GUILLÉN. Entre estos desnudos troncos
dos bultos se dejan ver. 2065

Yo me quiero retirar
adonde a la mira esté,
para atender sus acciones,
sin darle cuidado al Rey. *(Vase.)*

Salen Don Vicente y Chocolate.

VICENTE. Un hombre a la reja está. 2070

CHOCOLATE. Penante debe de ser
de una de tantas mondongas,
que hacen rastro a este vergel.

VICENTE. Retírate tú de aquí;
que solo podré más bien 2075
ocultarme, y ver si sale
Violante.

CHOCOLATE. Allí me estaré,
rogando a amor que salgamos
desta aventura con bien. *(Vase.)*

VICENTE. Para apurar sin testigos 2080
mis sospechas, le envié.
¡Qué fuera, válgame el cielo,
que este hombre fuera el Rey!

REINA. No mi ingenio encarezcáis
tanto.

REY. ¿Por qué no, si en él 2085
está demás el hablar,
y demás el parecer?

Llega Elvira a la reja.

ELVIRA. Todas las damas, señora,
buscándote vienen.

REINA. Pues
quitarme de aquí es fuerza, 2090
no se llegue esto a entender;
que pretendo proseguir
el engaño hasta saber
todos mis celos; que en fin
soy, aunque Reina, mujer. 2095

Sale Don Guillén.

GUILLÉN. Señor, la Reina he sentido
hablar por aquesta red,
y es fuerza que te retires.

REY. ¿Cuándo no ha sido cruel
para mí esta fiera?

REINA. Aora. 2100

REY. Dadme licencia.

REINA. ¿De qué?

REY. De hablaros aquí.

REINA. Sí doy:
de noche venir podréis.

REY. ¡O si nunca hubiera día!

ELVIRA. ¿Qué es aquesto?

REINA. ¿Qué ha de ser? 2105

Apurar una desdicha.
Ven, que yo te lo diré. *(Vanse.)*

Llega Don Vicente al Rey.

VICENTE. Juzgo que el hombre se va;
hablaron, nada escuché.

REY. Dichoso yo, que ya he visto 2110
un agrado, Don Guillén,
en esta ingrata; mañana
me manda la venga a ver.

VICENTE. ¡Válgame el cielo!

REY. (En la voz
desconozco a quien hablé.) 2115
¿Quién eres, hombre, a quién dije
mi secreto?

VICENTE. No sé quién;
mas soy quien sabrá guardalle.

REY. ¡Vive Dios que he de saber
quién eres!

VICENTE. Es imposible 2120
el dejarme conocer;
basta que sepa quien eres,
sin que tú sepas también
quien soy yo.

REY. Pues, ¿de qué modo,
dime, te has de defender? 2125

VICENTE. Desta suerte, pues no hay otras
armas, señor, contra un Rey.

REY. Seguiréte, aunque volando
vas.

Sale Don Guillén.

GULLÉN. ¿Qué es esto?

REY. Guillén,
a aquel hombre he de alcanzar. 2130

GULLÉN. Pues vamos los dos tras dél.

VICENTE. (Si el más acerado estoque
es de cera contra un Rey,
y la mayor valentía
volverle la espalda es, 2135
retirarme quiero aora.
Corazón, no hay que temer.
Quitaréme de delante,
porque el que alcanza mi fe,
diga que consigo lauros 2140
de valiente y de cortés.

JORNADA TERCERA

Salen el Rey y Don Guillén con capas de noche.

REY. Pues la noche oscura y fría
es a mi dulce querella
más que el día hermosa y bella,

más que nunca venga el día. 2145
Deje ya que en tal porfía
al más trémulo farol
venza su rubio arrebol,
sin que de la luz se valga,
y como la luna salga, 2150
más que nunca salga el sol.
A despecho, y a pesar
del oficio que le han dado,
duerma una vez sin cuidado
quien tiene a que madrugar; 2155
que menos no le han de echar
desde el lirio al girasol
las flores; que otro arrebol
es a ilustrallas bastante;
y como salga Violante, 2160
más que nunca salga el sol.

GUILLÉN. Con mudo silencio atento
estoy oyendo, señor,
por no estorbar a tu amor
las muestras de tu contento. 2165

REY. ¿Ves cuánto encarecimiento
hoy a repetir me obligo?
pues del sujeto que sigo,
el mérito menos grave,
en lo que digo no cabe, 2170
ni aun cabe en lo que no digo;
porque cuanta perfección
puso el cielo en su hermosura,
es pequeña cifra obscura
de su mucha discreción. 2175
Todo causa admiración:
los ojos allí rendidos

al verla yo, y repetidos
al oírla mis enojos,
se están muriendo mis ojos 2180
de envidia de mis oídos.
Yo culpé toda mi vida
a quien fea enamoró,
mas ya le disculpo yo,
si la fea es entendida. 2185
Y aunque haya causa que impida
mis dichas, siempre diré
que feliz mil veces fue
la primer noche que aquí
vine, Guillén, y la oí 2190
agradecida a mi fe;
pues desde ella continuado
siempre gocé este favor.

GUILLÉN. Bien presumí yo, señor,
que esta noche hubiera dado 2195
antes que placer, enfado,
por el hombre que seguimos.

REY. Nunca quién era supimos;
mas puesto que no volvió
otra noche, aunque tú y yo 2200
tanta diligencia hicimos
de examinar con cuidado
el puesto, por si volvía,
no he dudado que sería
algún hombre, que parado 2205
estaba acaso, y turbado
huyó al conocerme a mí.
¿Mas no abren la reja?

GUILLÉN. Sí.

REY. Bien te puedes retirar
donde sueles esperar. 2210

GULLÉN. No me quitaré de allí. *(Vase.)*

Sale la Reina a la reja.

REINA. Estará de mi tardanza
vuestra Magestad, señor,
quejoso.

REY. En mí fuera error,
estando con esperanza; 2215
que si esperando se alcanza
el bien de veros aquí,
dichoso aquel tiempo fui
que esperé, pues que troqué
la pena con que esperé 2220
de la gloria con que os vi.

REINA. Si tan bien entretenido
aquí, señor, os juzgara
con la esperanza, tardara
más en haber respondido; 2225
porque si el despique ha sido
de la pena que pasáis
ver la gloria que buscáis,
no siendo la gloria yo,
mal hice en venir, pues no 2230
os traigo lo que esperáis.

REY. Eso conocer no quiero,
pues sabe Amor, ciego dios,
que viene, Violante, en vos
toda la gloria que espero. 2235

REINA. No será estilo grosero
que crédito no haya dado,
aunque este nombre he escuchado.

REY. Desconfianzas dejemos,
que por aora tenemos 2240
que hablar con mayor cuidado.

REINA. ¿En cuidado, y mayor?

REY. Sí,
aunque distinto en los dos;
que es de placer para vos,
y de pesar para mí. 2245

REINA. ¿Cómo puede ser ansí?

REY. Como es que ya de volver
trata Don Vicente a os ver;
y que con vos ha de hablar.
Yo, pues tengo por pesar 2250
daros nuevas de placer.
Por una carta he sabido
suya, que apenas llegó,
cuando el moro ejecutó
las treguas con el partido, 2255
harto mi amor lo ha sentido.
De suerte que concluida
la campaña, y despedida
del ejército la gente,
estará aquí brevemente. 2260
Bien podéis, de agradecida
a nueva tan lisonjera,
dar en mi desconfianza
de albricias una esperanza;
pues si no me persuadiera 2265

a que viniendo él, me espera
la dicha de poder veros
en vuestra casa, y deberos
más de cerca este favor,
me hubiera muerto el dolor. 2270

REINA. A dos cosas responderos,
señor, me ha tocado: una,
en cuanto a lo que decís
de mi gusto, pues pedís
albricias a mi fortuna. 2275
A ésta digo que importuna
para mí esta nueva ha sido
tanto, que no os he debido
las albricias, pues jamás
he sentido cosa más, 2280
que su venida he sentido.
La otra, en cuanto a consolaros
de que venga; que en pensar
que en mi casa más lugar
tendré de veros y hablaros, 2285
también me da el escucharos
que sentir, porque no es
estilo noble y cortés,
digno de vos, que los cielos
traigan antes los consuelos 2290
librados para después.
Y así, de vos ofendida,
por veros tan consolado,
aun desto que aquí os he hablado,
no he de acordarme en mi vida. 2295
Si me habláis, desentendida
me hallaréis siempre, porque
jamás os confesaré
que os hablé, señor, ni os vi.

(¿Quién de dos pudiera así 2300
desesperar una fe?)

REY. Si yo, a precio de lograr
mi esperanza, dispusiera
de ajeno dueño, o quisiera
otro, debierais culpar 2305
mi consuelo en mi pesar,
siendo logro, aunque importuno;
pero ya, si sois de uno,
¿no podrá el ciego dios
que seamos dichosos dos? 2310

REINA. Fuera no serlo ninguno,
porque el querer y reinar
no ha de partirse.

REY. Si en mi...

(Cuchilladas dentro.)

GUILLÉN. No habéis de pasar de aquí.

CHOCOLATE. ¿Habrá más de no pasar? 2315

GUILLÉN. Más; que tengo de apurar
quién sois.

CHOCOLATE. ¡Ése es caso fuerte!

REY. Ruido oigo.

REINA. ¡Tirana suerte!

REY. Retiraos, que a saber voy. *(Vase.)*

REINA. ¡Mi Rey! ¡Señor! ¡Muerta soy! 2320

GUILLÉN. Aunque me rinda a la muerte,
tengo de saber quién eres.

Salen Don Guillén y el Rey.

REY. Yo te ayudaré.

GUILLÉN. Di el nombre.

REY. Don Guillén, yo soy, detente.

GUILLÉN. Embarazado contigo, 2325
ya el otro se desaparece.

REY. ¿Qué ha sido esto?

GUILLÉN. Retirado,
señor, estaba en las redes,
que guarnición de esmeralda
copados álamos tejen, 2330
cuando entre las pardas calles
de sus laberintos verdes,
vi dos hombres que seguían
la margen de las paredes.
Como vi que se acercaban 2335
donde hablabas, receléme;
y pretendiendo estorbarles
a un tiempo y reconocerles:
«No habéis de pasar de aquí»,
les dije, cuando valiente 2340
el uno y cobarde el otro,
uno huyó, y otro acomete.
Yo, partiendo en dos mitades
de acciones tan diferentes,

no pude seguir a aquél, 2345
todo ocupado con éste.
Al ruido viniste tú,
y él en viniendo más gente,
se retiró sin volver
la espalda; bien como suele 2350
el león, que despreciando
aun a los mismos que teme,
huye con valor; que huyendo
hay quien el ánimo muestre.

REY. Sin duda que es aquél mismo 2355
que yo hallé. El cuidado vuelve
a ser dos veces mayor,
ya repetido dos veces.
Diera por saber quién es
este hombre...

(Dentro, como cayendo en el tablado.)

CHOCOLATE. ¡Jesús mil veces! 2360

GUILLÉN. Uno desde aquel ribazo
cayó.

REY. Sin duda que es éste.

GUILLÉN. Muchos pensando que huyen
el riesgo, al riesgo se vuelven.

CHOCOLATE. ¡Que digan que es saludable 2365
el huir!

GUILLÉN. Hombre, detente.

CHOCOLATE. Más dificultoso fuera
el decirme que anduviese,

cuando, al tener ocho piernas,
me hubiera quebrado nueve. 2370

REY. Dime quién eres, o aquí
hoy a morir te resuelve.

CHOCOLATE. Siempre que a escoger me dan,
lo mejor escojo siempre.

REY. Pues muere, si es lo mejor 2375
el ostentar ser valiente.

CHOCOLATE. El ostentarme gallina
es muy mejor.

REY. Pues ¿quién eres?

CHOCOLATE. Un Chocolate, que aora
todo es cacao cuanto tiene. 2380

REY. ¿Qué hacías aquí?

CHOCOLATE. Con un hombre,
de quien soy leal sirviente,
vine, que nunca viniera.

REY. Y él ¿quién es?

CHOCOLATE. Él comunmente
Don Vicente para todos, 2385
para mí es Pero Vicente.

REY. ¿Don Vicente de Fox?

CHOCOLATE. Sí.

REY. Pues ¿está aquí?

CHOCOLATE. De las veinte
necedades españolas,
es ésta la necedad siete. 2390
¿Si no estuviese aquí, cómo
querías que aquí estuviese?

REY. ¿No estaba en Mallorca?

CHOCOLATE. Estaba;
pero como ya se vuelve,
después de la tregua hecha, 2395
a Zaragoza la gente,
se adelantó dos jornadas,
por sólo ver si pudiese
ver a su mujer primero
que al Rey; que es tan imprudente, 2400
que a ver su propia mujer,
corriendo postas se viene.
Quiso llegar a estas rejas,
y un gigante, descendiente
de Galafre, el que guardaba 2405
a un tiempo a Mantible el puente,
al paso se puso; y yo,
que de los estilos siempre
marciales me apiado más
del satírico que el fuerte, 2410
me entré a aqueste bosque huyendo,
si he de hablar cristianamente,
donde tahur de mí mismo,
paré, perdiendo la suerte
que corría en mi favor, 2415
y me he quebrado los dientes,
las narices y las piernas.
Y porque nada me quede
sano, dicen que han querido

que la cabeza me quiebre, 2420
contándoles mi tragedia.
Si otra cosa no me quieren,
yo sí, y es que entre los dos
un rato a cuestas me lleven
a un algebrista de viejo, 2425
que este cuerpo me remiende.

REY. Esto está peor que estaba,
Don Guillén, pues Don Vicente
fue el que yo aquí la primera
noche hablé.

GUILLÉN. Claro se infiere 2430
que se detendría al partirse,
quien se adelanta al volverse.

REY. Dar cuenta a Violante importa
de todo, para que piense,
avisada del suceso, 2435
lo que ha de hacer.

GUILLÉN. Un billete
le escribiré.

REY. A tanto empeño,
es muy tibio medio éste.
Yo he de hablarla.

GUILLÉN. ¿Cómo piensas
disponerlo?

REY. Desta suerte... 2440

CHOCOLATE. (¿Cuánto va, que están pensando
el modo de darme muerte?)

REY. Iré a la quinta diciendo
que salí a caza por este
monte, y que el sol me obligó 2445
con su saña a recogerme.
El cuarto está de Violante,
de la Reina al cuarto enfrente;
en él me entraré primero,
como que acaso sucede 2450
el yerro de entrarme en él;
que no será inconveniente,
pues la Reina deste amor
tan poca noticia tiene.
Y aun a más ha de pasar 2455
el lance a que he de atreverme,
porque una vez dentro, tengo
de procurar esconderme
en el aposento de uno
de sus jardineros; que este 2460
medio no será difícil
con despedirme y volverme,
teniéndole tú avisado.
Y como yo allá me quede,
haciendo tú aquesta noche 2465
las señas como otras veces,
al salir Violante a hablarme,
con el seguro que suele,
de que en la calle estoy, tengo
de lograr mi amor.

GUILLÉN. Advierte 2470
que a mucho te atreves.

REY. No es
amante el que no se atreve.
Vamos allá, pues.

GUILLÉN. ¿No miras,
que si el sol ha de ofrecerte
la disculpa, aún es de noche? 2475

REY. Dices bien; fuerza es que espere
a estar bien entrado el día.

CHOCOLATE. (¿Qué hablan éstos entre dientes?)

REY. Hombre, el dejarte con vida
a mi piedad agradece. 2480

CHOCOLATE. Seré de tan gran señor
escarpín eternamente.

REY. (¡Ay, bellísima Violante,
qué de pesares me debes!) *(Vanse.)*

CHOCOLATE. Yo hombres corteses he visto, 2485
pero no hombres más corteses.
¡Qué blandura de señores!
En sabiendo lo que quieren,
no hablarán una palabra
descompuesta, aunque les tuesten. 2490

Sale Don Vicente.

VICENTE. He estado mi honor buscando
y aquí Chocolate vuelve,
porque no encuentren con él,
y quién soy a nadie cuente.

CHOCOLATE. Preguntadores señores, 2495
si es que arrepentidos vienen
de haberme dejado vivo,
que no lo estoy consideren
tanto como ustedes piensan.

VICENTE. ¿Chocolate?

CHOCOLATE. Sí, ¿quién eres? 2500

VICENTE. Yo soy.

CHOCOLATE. ¿Quién?

VICENTE. ¿No me conoces,
necio, que soy Don Vicente?

CHOCOLATE. ¿Don Vicente? No lo creo.

VICENTE. ¿Adónde vas?

CHOCOLATE. Para verte,
por una luz.

VICENTE. Dime agora, 2505
¿qué te ha sucedido?

CHOCOLATE. Atiende:
cuando sacaste la espada,
sentí a las espaldas gente,
y porque no nos matasen
sin defensa ...

VICENTE. ¿Qué?

CHOCOLATE. Dejéte, 2510
y a detener a los otros
me fui animoso y valiente.
La fortuna, que la fiesta
guarda de los inocentes,
me dio tal valor, que todos 2515
a cuchilladas se vuelven.

VICENTE. ¿Pues cómo dijiste aquí
aora llegando a verme:
«preguntadores señores»?
De que infiero claramente 2520
que te preguntaron algo.

CHOCOLATE. Pues si no dejas que llegue
al fin con el caso.

VICENTE. Di.

CHOCOLATE. Quedando solo, arriméme
a descansar, y de una 2525
puerta salió entonces gente.

VICENTE. Pues ¿había puerta en el bosque?

CHOCOLATE. Supongo yo que la hubiese,
y llamo puerta a un portillo
que hacían los ramos. Halléme, 2530
en fin, de dos abrazado,
y en el pecho un pistolete.
«¿Quién eres?» me preguntó
uno dellos. Yo prudente
dije: «No lo he de decir, 2535
aunque me deis dos mil muertes.—
¿Qué hacéis aquí? dijo otro.—
Espulgarme a escuras.—Mientes.
Espúlgome a escuras yo,
como otros pintan al temple.— 2540
¿Quién es ése que acompañas?—
Yo no acompaño.» Y en este
punto disparó cruel
el de la pistola.

VICENTE. Tente.
¿Cómo no se oyó del fuego 2545
respuesta?

CHOCOLATE. Como sirviente
no era, no era respondón
el fuego; y el caso es ése,
que no dio lumbre; y pasando
al acero su inclemente 2550
furor, una puñalada,
que no pasó del piquete,
me tiró otro. «Muerto soy»,
dije, y lacayo de *requiem*,
me tendí en el suelo; y ellos, 2555
que ya por muerto me tienen,
se van presto. Del hallarme
tú, presumo que vuelven,
y digo, «preguntadores»,
por los dimes y dirétes. 2560

VICENTE. En fin, ¿de ti no supieron
que fuese yo, ni quién fuese?

CHOCOLATE. ¡Eso habían de saber
de mi boca!

VICENTE. ¡Qué leal eres!

CHOCOLATE. Aun si lo supieras bien, 2565
no dudo que lo dijeses.

VICENTE. Por lo menos, si lo hubieras
dicho, lo herraras dos veces
en no avisarme, porque
hecho el daño, lo remedie. 2570

CHOCOLATE. Digo que si hallares nunca
que yo tu nombre dijese,
me mates. (Mucho sintiera
que la palabra me acete.)

VICENTE. ¡Válgame Dios! ¿Qué he de hacer, 2575
cercado de tan crueles
imaginaciones locas
como a mi discurso ofenden?
La noche que volví aquí,
por si aquí saber pudiese 2580
si con la Reina quedaba
Violante, ¡cielos valedme!
hallé en la ventana al Rey;
y presumiendo que fuese
yo Don Guillén, me contó 2585
gozoso, ufano y alegre,
que estaba favorecido
de una ingrata beldad. Llegue
mi muerte antes que otra vez
sin olvidarlo lo acuerde. 2590
Desconocióme antes que
la nombrase; y yo prudente
di a la fuga confianza
los riesgos del conocerme.
Abrevióse la jornada 2595
a que fui; y cuando pretenden
mis ansias desengañarme,
mis penas satisfacerme,
volviendo más por fineza,
que por ... ¡Ay lengua! detente, 2600
no digas celos; que un hombre
no es justo que lo confiese.
Por fineza sólo digo,
a ver aquélla que hoy tiene,

árbitro de mi fortuna, 2605
todos mis males y bienes.
En el mismo punto hallo
a Don Guillén, porque aumente
fuerzas a fuerzas la duda,
visto el incendio dos veces. 2610
Mas ¿qué digo, indicio? Miento;
que aún el indicio más leve
no ha llegado a mi noticia.
Miente mi discurso, miente
mi imaginación, supuesto 2615
que tantos descargos tiene
en la razón apurados,
y en la verdad evidentes.
A buscarlos voy, Violante.
¡Plegue a Dios que los encuentre! 2620
Dejo aparte los abonos
de quien soy y ser quien eres.
Haz, honor, que aquesta loca
imaginación me deje.
Chocolate, a mí me importa, 2625
supuesto que ya amanece,
y a ver a Violante vine,
que aora en la quinta entres,
y la digas a Violante
que pues que su cuarto tiene 2630
una puerta a los jardines,
la abra, y yo secretamente
entraré a verla primero
que a noticia del Rey llegue
que me he adelantado.

CHOCOLATE. Iré 2635
cuidadoso y diligente.

VICENTE. Escucha, pues tan bien sabes
callar, cuando a verla entres,
no digas lo que ha pasado.

CHOCOLATE. Callarélo, aunque reviente. *(Vase.)* 2640

VICENTE. A disimular, desdichas,
vamos. Haced que no llegue,
cielos, Violante a saber
que en mí cupo la más leve
desconfianza, porque 2645
propias y atentas mujeres,
es decirlas que se atrevan
el decirlas que las temen. *(Vase.)*

Salen la Reina y Elvira.

REINA. No he podido sosegar,
vacilando y discurriendo 2650
en qué ha podido parar
de aquella pendencia el riesgo.

ELVIRA. Ya se dijera, si hubiera
novedad.

REINA. Yo estoy muriendo.

ELVIRA. Siempre estuve mal, señora, 2655
yo con este fingimiento.
Muchas veces lo escuché,
y aunque nunca quise verlo,
tus temores no entendí.

REINA. Pues tanto me apuras, quiero 2660
que sepas cuantas razones
hoy en mi disculpa tengo.

Yo adoro al Rey de la suerte
que él me aborrece; que opuestos
nuestros dos hados, tomaron 2665
en la partición que hicieron
del patrimonio de estrellas,
los dos contrarios extremos,
todo el amor uno, y otro
todo el aborrecimiento. 2670
Esto asentado, y también
asentado, que tenemos
nuestras pasiones los Reyes,
al primer discurso vuelvo.
Acaso llegué a una reja 2675
del jardín ... Ya sabes esto:
que me habló el Rey por Violante;
que yo curiosa, queriendo
volver en el desengaño
fingí la voz; aunque es cierto 2680
que no había, para qué, ni hubo
menester fingirla, puesto
que della tenían tan muertas
las noticias sus despegos.
Luego si yo con fingir 2685
que soy la que adora, tengo
su imaginación burlada,
parado su pensamiento,
mi respeto asegurado,
pacíficos mis recelos, 2690
no ha sido culpable, Elvira,
de todo mi fingimiento.
Tan poca victoria ha sido
traerle aqueste rendimiento;
pues cuando se desengañe, 2695
conocerá, por lo menos,
que vista sin ceño, partes

para ser querida tengo.
Y aún no sé, Elvira, no sé
si diga, súpleme esto 2700
mi modestia, que he pensado
desengañarle, creyendo
que por aqueste camino
me ha de hacer merced el cielo
de cumplirme una palabra, 2705
que aunque me la ha dado en sueños,
para que el cielo la cumpla,
basta ser suya en efeto.

ELVIRA. Aunque no hallen hoy, señora,
conveniencia sus deseos 2710
en el desengaño, ya
fuerza ha de ser, pues ya creo
que ha de venir Don Vicente,
según tú dices, muy presto;
y en faltando desta quinta 2715
Violante, será muy cierto
que allá la busque, y que allá
se desengañe.

REINA. Primero
pensaré yo el mejor modo
de declararme.

ELVIRA. Habla quedo, 2720
que sale al jardín Violante.

REINA. Pues vente conmigo, haciendo
que no la ves; que aunque ella
no es culpa de mi tormento,
es de mi tormento causa, 2725
y como tal, verla siento. *(Vanse.)*

Salen Violante y Leonor.

VIOLANTE. ¿Abriste la puerta?

LEONOR. Sí.

VIOLANTE. Pues el jardín recorriendo
anda; no le vean entrar.
¡Gracias al amor, que llego 2730
a ver tan felice día!
Dos dichas a un tiempo tengo:
una el venir Don Vicente,
y otra el venir de secreto,
haciendo fineza el verme. 2735
Loca me tiene el contento;
y más cuando sus pesares
tan pacíficos y quietos
ha de hallar, pues en su ausencia
aun sola una acción no ha hecho 2740
el Rey de amor, que le dé
un cuidadoso recelo.

Salen Don Vicente y Chocolate.

CHOCOLATE. A la puerta de su cuarto
te espera.

VICENTE. (Cobarde llego,
porque no sé si sabré 2745
disimular mi tormento.)

VIOLANTE. Apenas Chocolate
habló aquí con Leonora,
que es quien me asiste aora,
cuando sin que dilate 2750
un solo instante el verte,
a recibirte salgo desta suerte.

Mi bien, señor, esposo,
seas tan bien venido,
como esperado has sido 2755
deste pecho amoroso,
que con amantes lazos, *(Abrázanse.)*
feliz te espera en sus dichosos brazos.

VICENTE. Tú seas, dueño mío,
mil veces bien hallada, 2760
como has sido deseada
deste preso albedrío,
que en alas ha volado
de amor, por llegar presto y abrasado.
Apenas, acabadas 2765
las treguas de la guerra,
pisé la amada tierra,
cuando a largas jornadas,
fino amante y sujeto
a verte me adelanto de secreto. 2770

VIOLANTE. Aunque esté a la fineza
con que a verme has venido
mi pecho agradecido,
no sé con qué tibieza
me hablas, me oyes, me miras, 2775
y hacia dentro con temor suspiras,
que das al pensamiento.
Cuando más se aconseja,
causa de que haya queja
del agradecimiento. 2780
¿Con qué cuidado vienes?
Mi bien, ¿qué traes? Di, mi bien, ¿qué [tienes?

VICENTE. (¿Pudieran ser fingidos
tan bien dichos enojos?

Nada habéis visto, ojos ; 2785
mucho escucháis, oídos.
No queda en mi confuso devaneo
lo que imagino más que lo que veo.)
Del camino cansado,
y no bueno he venido. 2790
Ésta la causa ha sido;
no ha sido desagrado,
señora, el suspenderme.

VIOLANTE. Lo peor es que pudiste responderme;
porque cuando trajeras 2795
algunas pesadumbres,
del tiempo a las costumbres
dejara, las vencieras.
Esto yo te lo fío;
mas la salud no puedo, dueño mío. 2800
¡Pluguiera a Dios, pluguiera
que a costa de la mía!
hasta el alma este día
en albricias te diera;
y díganlo mis ojos, 2805
que lágrimas te ofrecen por despojos.

VICENTE. (Aora es tiempo, aora,
ilusión mal nacida,
de darte por vencida.
Violante es la que llora; 2810
no dirás más verdad, ¿qué estoy dudando?
imaginando tú, y ella llorando.)
Calla, Violante mía,
cuando muerto viniera,
sólo el verte me diera 2815
más vida, más placer, más alegría
que desearme puedes.

Todo en sólo ese llanto lo concedes.
Dame otra vez los brazos.

VIOLANTE. Pues que mi llanto pudo 2820
estrechar deste nudo
los amorosos lazos,
y a ser agradecida
la continua tarea de la vida;
ni cesará un instante 2825
de llorar mi fortuna.

VICENTE. No habrá risa ninguna,
bellísima Violante,
si el sol continuo llora.

Sale Leonor.

LEONOR. Señor...

VICENTE. Di.

LEONOR. ¡Muerta vengo!

VIOLANTE. ¿Qué hay, Leono-
[ra? 2830

LEONOR. El Rey...

VICENTE. ¡Qué mal empiezas!

VIOLANTE. Prosigue.

LEONOR. Aquesta mañana...
así lo oí...

VICENTE. No te turbes.

LEONOR. Salió...

VICENTE. ¿Qué dudas?

LEONOR. A caza.

VIOLANTE. ¿Qué ha sucedido?

LEONOR. Que 2835
huyendo del sol la saña,
contra el rigor de sus rayos,
de aquesta quinta se ampara,
y en ella ha entrado.

VICENTE. Pues bien,
¿qué novedad es extraña, 2840
que el Rey entre en esta quinta,
siendo esta quinta su casa?
Si es temor de que me vea
en su cuarto, más guardada
mi persona estará en éste. 2845

LEONOR. Si él en su cuarto se entrara,
aunque fuera novedad,
lo fuera sin circunstancia;
pero antes que hacia el cuarto
de la Reina...

VICENTE. Dilo.

VIOLANTE. Acaba. 2850

LEONOR. Viene a este cuarto.

VICENTE. ¿Qué dices?

VIOLANTE. Pues ¿de qué, señor, te espantas?
Si viene huyendo del sol,
¿qué mucho (¡alentemos alma!)
que por no ver a la Reina, 2855
aquí se entre?

VICENTE. Pues no extrañas
tan gran visita, no dudo
que esto muchas veces pasa.

VIOLANTE. No sólo pasó otra vez,
mas no le he visto la cara 2860
desde que tú te ausentaste,
ni le he hablado una palabra;
y así, no presumas...

VICENTE. Tente,
porque no presumo nada;
que si algún extremo ha hecho, 2865
necio el color de mi cara,
es, señora, de temer
que me halla aquí, ¡pena rara!
antes de haberle besado
la mano, y de mi jornada 2870
dándole cuenta, trayendo
la gente que se me encarga.

VIOLANTE. Pues retírate de aquí,
que es su condición extraña.
No te diga algún desaire. 2875

VICENTE. Fuerza será que lo haga...
(No tanto por eso, como
porque otro indicio no haya
contra mí, de que yo fui
el de las noches pasadas.) 2880

LEONOR. Ea, presto, que ya llega.

VICENTE. Chocolate, aquí te aparta,
porque podrá, si te ve,
discurrir con justa causa
ser el criado de anoche. 2885

CHOCOLATE. Si yo no hablé una palabra,
y era a escuras.

VICENTE. Ven conmigo.
(Cielos, la suerte está echada.
Tened lástima de mí;
que va en perderla o ganarla. 2890
Mas poco diré, aunque diga
fama, honor, ser, vida y alma.)

Escóndense detrás del paño.

VIOLANTE. No me pesa, aunque es tan grande
el empeño que me aguarda,
que esté Don Vicente donde 2895
pueda las verdades claras
oir de mi amor, pues verá
en lo que aquí el Rey me habla,
que desesperado o cuerdo,
no me ha hablado una palabra. 2900

Sale el Rey.

REY. ¿Tendréis a gran novedad,
bella Violante, que haga
estos extremos de amor?

VIOLANTE. Sí, gran señor, y admirada
estoy de que entréis aquí, 2905

cosa a vos tan poco usada,
y en mí tan poco advertida;
y cualquiera acción se extraña
la primera vez que os veo.

REY. Decís bien.

VICENTE. (Albricias, alma, 2910
que entra bien el desengaño;
quiera Dios que tan bien salga.)

REY. Pero las leyes se rompen,
cuando es precisa la causa;
y la que hoy me arroja a entrar 2915
aquí, sin mirar en nada,
es tal, que no me es posible,
bella Violante, escusalla;
que donde tu vida importa,
¿qué extremo habrá que no haga? 2920

VIOLANTE. ¿Mi vida, señor?

REY. Tu vida;
y antes que digas palabra,
dime, ¿has visto a Don Vicente?

VIOLANTE. (Él con cólera y con rabia
le busca, por eso dice 2925
que me va la vida.)

REY. Habla;
¿hasle visto?

VIOLANTE. No, señor.

REY. Con esto está confirmada

mi sospecha y tu peligro.
Oye, y sabrás lo que pasa. 2930
Anoche cuando a la reja
hablando contigo estaba...

VIOLANTE. ¿Conmigo anoche a la reja?
¡Ya más desdichas me aguardan!

REY. No te hagas desentendida; 2935
que aunque juraste enojada
negar siempre los favores
que te debieron mis ansias,
no es tiempo de que los cumplas.

VIOLANTE. ¿Yo? ¿cómo? ¿cuándo (¡turbada 2940
estoy!) hablé, juré? ¿Cuándo?

REY. Ya los disimulos bastan;
mas diga yo a lo que vengo,
y tú, sabiendo la causa,
verás si te está mejor 2945
negarla que confirmarla.

VICENTE. (¿Hay más penas?)

VIOLANTE. (¿Hay más desdichas?)

REY. Anoche pues, cuando hablaba
por esta reja contigo,
el ruido de cuchilladas... 2950

VICENTE. (¿Hay hombre más infeliz?)

VIOLANTE. (¿Hay mujer más desdichada?)

REY. Yo a saber lo que era fui,

vi a Don Guillén, que intentaba
conocer a un hombre, como 2955
la primera vez que humana
me escuchaste.

VIOLANTE. Yo, señor,
jamás te escuché.

VICENTE. (¡Ha ingrata!)

REY. El hombre se nos perdió
entre las sombras y ramas; 2960
pero hallamos un criado.

CHOCOLATE. (Aora entro yo en la danza.)

REY. Que dijo que Don Vicente
aquí de secreto estaba.

VICENTE. Tú me has vendido.

CHOCOLATE. No he hecho, 2965
que por ti no dieron blanca.

REY. Que había venido a verte,
dijo, y pues de verte falta,
sus recelos le han traído;
yo, temiendo tu desgracia, 2970
te vengo a ofrecer...

Sale Don Guillén, turbado.

GUILLÉN. Señor,
haciendo lo que me mandas
con el jardinero, he visto
desde aquesta verde estancia

que la Reina mi señora, 2975
de que aquí estás informada,
ha salido de su cuarto,
y a verte a este cuarto pasa.

REY. (¿Qué aun para hablar de desdichas
no dé tiempo esta tirana?) 2980

VIOLANTE. (¿Qué aun para satisfacer
no den lugar mis desgracias?)

VICENTE. (¿Qué aun para matar, no apuren
todo el veneno mis ansias?)

CHOCOLATE. (¿Qué aun para mentir, no tenga 2985
yo ni ventura ni gracia?)

Sale la Reina.

REINA. (Ya del riesgo de la noche,
viendo al Rey, asegurada,
habré de fingir de día,
pues la noche no me basta.) 2990
Vuestra Magestad, señor,
una vez que acaso pasa
los umbrales desta quinta,
¡tanto en dejarse ver tarda!

REY. Por ese monte salí 2995
a caza aquesta mañana;
hízome el sol retirar,
e imaginando que estaba
en este cuarto tu Alteza,
entré en él por ignorancia. 3000

REINA. No me espanto que ignoréis

las viviendas desta casa,
que las visitáis muy poco;
y ya, señor, que os engaña
la imaginación, pues ciega 3005
a unas busca, y a otras halla.
Por si acaso os sucediere
otra vez, sabed la casa.
Este cuarto es de Violante,
que estos días me acompaña. 3010
Venid, y sabréis el mío.

REY. (Fuerza es que con ella vaya
por no confesarlo todo.)
Aunque declina y desmaya
ya el sol, y he de volverme 3015
luego, haré lo que me manda
vuestra Alteza.

REINA. (¡Quién creyera,
que una imaginación haga
que se aborrezca de día
lo que de noche se ama!) 3020

REY. Don Guillén, dile a Violante
que si ha fingido, por causa
del enojo, o de guardarse
de una de aquellas criadas,
que no deje aquesta noche 3025
de hablarme donde me hable.

REINA. ¿No venís, señor?

REY. Ya voy.

REINA. (Ni aun Don Guillén ha de hablarla.)

REY. (¡Quién pudiera hacer, Violante,
que la Reina, ¡pena extraña! 3030
tuviera tu discreción,
ya que la beldad le falta!)

VIOLANTE. (¿Quién en el mundo se ha visto
en igual riesgo empeñada?)

VICENTE. Ya que de imaginación 3035
mi pena a evidencias pasa,
saldré y daréle la muerte,
ya que ha vuelto el Rey la espalda.

Vanse entrando, y desde la puerta la Reina vuelve a llamar a Violante, estando Don Vicente con la daga empuñada.

REINA. Violante.

VIOLANTE. Señora.

REINA. Ven
conmigo.

VIOLANTE. Pues ¿qué me mandas? 3040

REINA. Tengo que hablarte; no quedes
sola, hasta que el Rey se vaya.

VIOLANTE. Siempre yo he de obedecerte.

LEONOR. (Y nunca de mejor gana.)

VIOLANTE. (Suspendióse mi desdicha.) 3045

VICENTE. (Dilatóse mi venganza.)

CHOCOLATE. ¡Qué diera aora yo por
que la Reina me llamara
a mí también!

(Vase la Reina, y con ella Violante.)

VICENTE. Tú, villano,
has sido de todo causa. 3050

CHOCOLATE. ¿Pues soy yo el Rey, o Violante,
o la Reina, o la ventana,
o la noche del jardín?

VICENTE. Mataréte a puñaladas.

CHOCOLATE. No me puedo detener 3055
a recibirlas, que llama
la Reina. *(Vase.)*

VICENTE. Salir no puedo
tras él; tú, Leonor, aguarda.

LEONOR. ¿No ves que siempre me toca
el ir donde va mi ama? *(Vase.)* 3060

VICENTE. Solo me han dejado. ¡Cielos!
¿qué haré cercado de tantas
penas y desdichas juntas?
Mas no hay que pensar en nada,
vacilar sin discurrir. 3065
Violante y el Rey me agravian;
y pues no puedo tomar
más que la media venganza,
muera Violante, el Rey viva.
A lo que desde aquí alcanza 3070
mi vista, ya el Rey se va.

No dudo que esta tirana
en el cuarto de la Reina
se esconda, evidencia es clara;
pues, que no ha de osar venir 3075
donde la muerte la aguarda.
Pues ¿qué he de hacer? Ya lo sé.
En las ruinas derribadas,
que parte de este jardín
tiene, he de ocultarme, hasta 3080
que la noche dé ocasión
para salir a lograrla.
Para que a este cuarto vuelva,
abriré esta puerta falsa,
y entrando en él esta noche 3085
por una de sus ventanas,
la daré la muerte. Agora,
caducas piedras y ramas,
dadme sepulcro vosotras;
que no será acción tirana 3090
sepultarme vivo, puesto
que voy cadáver con alma. *(Vase.)*

VIOLANTE. Fuese el Rey, y retirada
la Reina a su cuarto, yo
sola he quedado. ¿Nació 3095
alguna más desdichada?
No, porque la más airada
suerte que el hado contiene,
rigor que el cielo previene,
desdicha que el tiempo ordena, 3100
es que uno tenga la pena
de la culpa que no tiene.
Mas digo mal, pues prevengo
yo de mi estrella disculpa
el ver que no tengo culpa 3105

de la pena ¡ay Dios! que tengo.
En esto sólo a hallar vengo
consuelo: de que inferí
nuevo tormento, pues vi
que lo que por tantos modos 3110
es despecho para todos,
es consuelo para mí.
Honor, ¿qué he de hacer? Si intento
volver a mi cuarto hoy,
dispuesta a mi muerte voy; 3115
si temerosa me ausento,
añado otro fundamento.
Ir es desesperación;
no ir, confirmar traición.
Razón tengo ...no equivale; 3120
pues si no hay cosa que iguale,
¿qué importa tener razón?
¡Ay, mi esposo! si mi vida
remedio a tu daño diera,
contenta yo a morir fuera 3125
sacrificada y rendida;
pero que mi muerte impida
me dice a voces mi honor,
porque a ti te está mejor,
hasta que tengas bastante 3130
desengaño.

Sale el Conde.

CONDE. ¿Qué hay, Violante?
¿por qué das voces?

VIOLANTE. Señor...

CONDE. ¿Qué tienes?

VIOLANTE. Un dolor fiero.

CONDE. Pues ¿de qué nace?

VIOLANTE. No sé.

CONDE. Cuéntamele.

VIOLANTE. No podré. 3135

CONDE. ¿Por qué?

VIOLANTE. Porque muda muero.

CONDE. Remedio habrá.

VIOLANTE. No le espero.

CONDE. ¿Cómo?

VIOLANTE. Como estoy sintiendo.

CONDE. ¿Qué es?

VIOLANTE. Absorta me suspendo.

CONDE. ¿Qué es esto?

VIOLANTE. Estrella inconstante. 3140

CONDE. No te entiendo.

VIOLANTE. No te espante,
que yo tampoco me entiendo.

CONDE. Yendo a tu cuarto a buscarte,
abierto y solo le vi,

y viniendo a verte aquí, 3145
quisiera irme sin hablarte;
porque llegando a mirarte
con tan grande turbación,
no quisiera la ocasión
apurar, por no saber 3150
si te puede suceder
una desesperación.
Al Rey en el bosque vía,
sin que me viese; advertí
que hacia la quinta, ¡ay de mí! 3155
segunda vez se volvía.
No discurro en qué sería
la causa. Y llegando a verte,
Violante, así desta suerte,
temo cualquiera desdicha. 3160
Pues en nada tengo dicha,
llegue ya el fin de mi muerte.
Háblame claro.

VIOLANTE. Señor,
¿tú no eres mi padre?

CONDE. Sí.

VIOLANTE. ¿Creerás que heredé de ti 3165
sangre, lustre, ser y honor?

CONDE. Siempre creeré lo mejor.

VIOLANTE. Pues yo soy tan desdichada
que, de una culpa imputada,
mi muerte tengo presente. 3170
Si así teme una inocente,
¿cómo teme una culpada?

Sabe el cielo que no he dado
a mi desdicha ocasión
con la más pequeña acción; 3175
ella se ha facilitado.
Don Vicente, que ha llegado
de secreto, ha presumido...
pero digo mal; ha oído
que yo le puedo ofender. 3180
¿Quién podrá satisfacer
cara a cara a un ofendido,
que contra sí mismo piensa
con razón o sin razón?
pues darle satisfacción, 3185
es acordarle la ofensa.
Mi confusión es inmensa,
porque aunque mi gran lealtad
verdad es, es la crueldad
del lance tal, que en favor 3190
mío dos veces, señor,
es desnuda mi verdad.
Si yo alcanzara o supiera
por dónde me viene el daño,
a buscar el desengaño 3195
por los mismos pasos fuera;
pero viene de manera
oculto y disimulado,
que por adonde ha pasado
aún la huella se divisa. 3200
Tan ligeramente pisa
el ladrón de mi cuidado.

CONDE. Violante, a mí me está bien
creer tus satisfacciones;
pero al riesgo a que te pones, 3205
has de creer tú también.

Si no estás culpada, en quien
tu desdicha ocasionó
yo me vengaré; mas no
si lo estás.

VIOLANTE. Lo mismo dice 3210
mi voz: muera de infelice,
pero de culpada no.

CONDE. ¿Dónde Don Vicente está?

VIOLANTE. En mi cuarto le dejé.

CONDE. Solo y abierto le hallé; 3215
que dél se ha ausentado ya.
Vamos a él los dos.

VIOLANTE. ¿Yo allá?

CONDE. Sí; ¿qué temes?

VIOLANTE. No el castigo,
la violencia.

CONDE. Yo me obligo
a pasar esta violencia. 3220
¿Va contigo tu inocencia?

VIOLANTE. Sí.

CONDE. Pues ven aora conmigo. *(Vanse.)*

Salen por distintos lados, sin verse el uno al otro, el Rey y Don Vicente; uno muy triste, y otro muy alegre.

VICENTE. Ya que la noche ha bajado
llena de sombras y horror...

REY. Ya que enamorado dél, 3225
se va tras el día el sol...

VICENTE. Atreverme a salir quiero
desta parte adonde estoy.

REY. Del pobre albergue saldré,
que un jardinero me dio. 3230

VICENTE. ¿Habrá hombre más infeliz
en todo el mundo que yo?

REY. ¿Habrá más dichoso hombre,
si logro aquesta ocasión?

VICENTE. Ya Violante habrá a su cuarto 3235
vuelto, viendo que faltó
mi persona dél.

REY. Ya presto
Don Guillén, pues me dejó
a este efecto en el jardín,
vendrá a hacer la seña.

VICENTE. Hoy 3240
mi honor tengo de vengar.

REY. Hoy lograré su favor.

VICENTE. Que aunque el cuarto está cerrado,
entraré por un balcón.

REY. Que aunque tan desatendida 3245
hoy en su cuarto me habló,

quizá de alguna criada
entonces se recató,
y no dudo que vendrá.

VICENTE. A morir matando voy; 3250
mas si una vez entro dentro,
con despecho en el valor...

REY. Y si aquí una vez la veo,
confiado en la traición...

VICENTE. La tengo de dar la muerte. 3255

REY. La he de rendir a mi amor.

(Seña dentro.)

VICENTE. La seña en la reja han hecho,
que es la de aquel mirador
que al terrero cae.

REY. Ya hizo
Guillén la seña.

VICENTE. Mejor 3260
me sucede, pues si ella
a esta seña que llamó
responde, dará en mis manos.

REY. ¡O, quiera el vendado dios,
que respondiendo a la seña 3265
dé en manos de mi afición!

Vuelven cada uno por su puerta, y salen la Reina y Elvira.

REINA. ¿Hicieron la seña?

ELVIRA. Sí.

REINA. Pues que ya resuelta estoy
a declararme, que espera
el Rey adonde me habló, 3270
tú, por lo que sucediere,
con toda la prevención
de luz y gente estarás,
y sal, si oyeres mi voz.

Vase Elvira, y la Reina se acerca como a oscuras a la reja.

REINA. ¿Quién, cielos, creerá en el mundo 3275
de mí, que siendo quien soy,
en aquestos pasos ande?
Mas ¿qué digo? que es error;
pues cuantas a sus esposos
los quisieren como yo, 3280
procurarán divertirles
de cualquier ajeno amor.
El ser Reina en este caso
será pequeña objeción;
que amor es alma, y las almas 3285
Reinas, no vasallas son.
Créalo la que lo hiciere,
cuando lea mi pasión,
por historia celebrada
de las victorias de amor. 3290

VICENTE. (Ya a la ventana se acerca
mi enemiga. ¡Qué rigor!)

REY. (Ya viene hacia la ventana.
¡Qué dicha!)

(Seña otra vez.)

REINA. ¡Turbada estoy!

VICENTE. (¿Quién mayor disgusto tuvo?) 3295

REY. (¿Quién tuvo gusto mayor?)

VICENTE. (¿Qué espero? Voy a matarla.)

REY. (¿Qué aguardo? A abrazarla voy.)

VICENTE. (Esta vez, Violante ingrata,
esta vez ...)

Llegan los dos; y viéndose el uno al otro, se apartan y sacan las espadas, y el Rey se pone delante de la Reina.

REINA. ¡Válgame Dios! 3300
Hombres, ¿quién sois? ¡Ay de mí!

VICENTE. Quien te dará muerte hoy.

REY. Yo quien te dará la vida.

REINA. ¿Cómo estáis aquí los dos?

VICENTE. Como yo vengo a tomar 3305
de mi honor satisfacción.

REY. Y yo vengo a defenderte.

VICENTE. No podrás ...

REINA. ¡Qué confusión!

VICENTE. Porque es un rayo mi espada.

REY. ¿Hazme conocido?

VICENTE. No. 3310

REY. Huélgome, porque el respeto
no haga lo que hará el dolor.

VICENTE. Mi obligación es morir,
cumpliendo mi obligación.
Sed testigos, cielos, que 3315
tiro a Violante, al Rey no.

REINA. ¡Muerta estoy! No sé qué hacer.

Dentro Don Guillén, el Conde y Violante dentro por otra parte; y Elvira saca luces por en medio dellos, y salen todos los demás.

GUILLÉN. Ruido en el jardín se oyó.

ELVIRA. Aunque la Reina no llame,
sacad luces, que hay traición. 3320

REY. ¿Qué miro? ¡Válgame el cielo!
¿Qué veo? ¡Válgame Dios!

VICENTE. ¿Vos sois con quien yo reñía?
¿Y por quien reñía sois vos?
¡Quién muchas vidas tuviera, 3325
que dar en satisfacción
deste ciego atrevimiento!
Una tengo, aquesta os doy.

(De rodillas, y arroja la espada.)

REY. ¿Cómo? ¿Vuestra Alteza es quien
aquí estaba?

REINA. Sí, yo soy 3330
la que partiendo su suerte
entre la luna y el sol,
de vos adorada vive,
y aborrecida de vos.
Con el nombre de Violante 3335
os hablé por el balcón.
De mí estáis enamorado
de noche, si de día no.
Pues una mentira, Rey,
tanta pasión os debió, 3340
¿por qué una verdad no puede
deber la misma pasión?
Mirad, que será defecto
de una real condición,
el que pueda la mentira 3345
más que la verdad con vos.
Violante me imaginasteis;
aunque veis que no lo soy,
amad, señor, por acierto
lo que amasteis por error. 3350
En publicar este engaño
no se embaraza mi voz,
porque tiene por disculpa
el ser nacido de amor.
Si una imaginación sola 3355
finezas os mereció,
y ésa misma a Don Vicente
tantos pesares costó,
haga caso aquesta vez,
con que me hallaréis, señor, 3360
olvidada de mi estrella,

asunto digno de vos.
Y él en su esposa hallará
desengaño de su honor,
para que conozca el mundo 3365
en la historia de los dos,
que el *gusto y disgusto*
desta vida *son*
no más que una leve
imaginación. 3370

REY. (Aunque pudiera ofenderme
deste padecido error,
con la que hablé se halla ya
en pena de mi pasión.
Y además desto, pendiente 3375
de Violante está el honor,
de Don Vicente y el Conde.
Justo es dar satisfacción;
pues acudamos a todo,
que yo valgo más que yo.) 3380
Alzad, señora, del suelo,
que sólo corrido estoy
de que por otra os amé,
mereciéndolo por vos.
Del engaño que me hicisteis, 3385
mi brazo dará el perdón;
y a vos también, Don Vicente,
del desacierto os le doy;
que si lo que imaginasteis
a este lance os obligó, 3390
y lo que yo imaginé
también me empeñó a esta acción,
vuestro gusto y mi disgusto,
puesto que tan unos son,
es bien que se den las manos, 3395

publicando en alta voz
que el *gusto y disgusto*
desta vida *son*
no más que una leve
imaginación. 3400

VICENTE. Dame mil veces las plantas;
y tú, Violante, mi error
perdona.

VIOLANTE. ¡Gracias al cielo
que te miro sin temor!

CONDE. Dicha fue que me quedara 3405
contigo esta noche yo,
porque no se dilatase
este gusto a mi afición.

REY. En la corte, Don Vicente,
donde con la Reina voy, 3410
me contaréis la jornada.

REINA. ¡Dichosa mil veces yo!

CHOCOLATE. Ésta es verdadera historia,
de que saque el pío lector,
que se estime lo que es propio; 3415
que lo ajeno no es mejor.
Pues como imagina un hombre,
que todas mujeres son,
y que no es mejor ninguna,
porque cualquiera es peor, 3420
con la suya vivirá
contento. Pues lo enseñó
la comedia, imaginad,

si os dio disgusto, que os dio
gusto; y con esto dirá 3425
agradecido el autor
que el *gusto y disgusto*
desta vida *son*
no más que una leve
imaginación. 3430

PART III

LIST OF VARIANTS

LIST OF VARIANTS

The following abbreviations have been used for the list of variants:

P	*Princeps* Edition	(1657)
VT	Vera Tassis Edition	(1694)

The complete title of P is as follows:

LA GRAN COMEDIA
DE GUSTOS, Y DISGUSTOS
SON NO MAS QUE IMAGINACION.
DE DON PEDRO CALDERON.

The complete title of VT includes a few more lines:

LA GRAN COMEDIA,
GUSTOS, Y DISGUSTOS
SON NO MAS QUE IMAGINACION.

Fiesta que se representó a sus
Magestades en el Salon de su
Real Palacio.

	P	VT
	PERSONAS.	PERSONAS QUE HABLAN EN ELLA.
	El Rey Don Pedro. *El Conde Monforte.* *Doña Violante dama.* *Elvira dama.* *La Reyna Doña Maria.* *Leonor dueña.* *Don Guillen.* *Don Vicente.* *Chocolate gracioso.*	*Don Pedro, Rey de Aragon.* *Doña Violante, Dama.* *Don Vicente.* *Leonor, Dueña.* *El Conde Monforte.* *Don Guillen.* *Chocolate, gracioso.* *La Reyna Doña Maria.* *Doña Violante, Dama.* *Elvira, Dama.* *Criados, y acompañamiento.*
	Salen por una puerta el Conde, y Violante su hija,	*Sale por una puerta el Conde, y su hija Doña Violante,*
3.	estacion	estancia
12.	rosas	plantas
19.	estancia	mansion
31.	de	de la
39.	ve	lee
58.	y inquieta	e inquieta
58+.	There is no stage direction.	*Como entre sueños dice la Reina.*
66+.	This line is missing.	*Elvira.* Es Violante de Cardona.
81.	soñarla,	contarla, (This response seems more logical.)
98.	lleno	llena
103.	enamorada	enamorado
121.	*Rey.*	*Rey dentro.*

	P	VT
124.	*Vicente.*	*Vicente dentro.*
144.	una	a una
145.	Pero el caso fue,	El caso fue, pues,
157+.	traen	que traen
183.	vidas	vida
187.	adonde	donde
191.	desdicha	dichosa
195.	¿Yo?	Ya
197.	ningun riesgo	riesgo ninguno
212.	caida	causa
221.	despreciar	despreciarla
223.	es	que es
229.	Mompiller,	Mompeller,
234.	Pos	Por
235.	en casa hablar del	hable aqui dél
247.	marido	esposo
253.	adbitro	arbitrio
263.	embidia	embidias
269.	me	no
278.	vencerlas.	vencerla.
279.	Probando	Pues cuando
306.	cerca	acerca
308.	está hecha	hecha está
323.	a la reyna, pues	la reyna, porque
325.	There is no stage direction.	*Aparte.*
335.	en	con
347.	en vano	vano
377.	todo.	todo virtud.
384.	y si	que si
387-436.		This entire passage is omitted.
443.	pagas,	apagas,

	P	VT
465.	velado	he velado
510.	muy	y muy
511.	enemigo,	mi enemigo,
515.	*(Que aun ni,* being more logical, is used in the annotated edition.)	que aun
534.	midiendose	rindiendose
546.	ahunarse	a unarse
548.	infelize	infeliz
564.	yo	y
572.	la	aquesta
572+.	*Sale Don Vicente, y Chocolate escuchando.*	*Sale Don Vicente, y Chocolate como escuchando.*
609.	se	le
612.	hablar.	hablarte. (This change disrupts the metric form of the *espinela.)*
620.	nuestro	a nuestro
675.	viviamos,	vivimos,
678.	recelos.	celos.
688.	me	si me
714.	pues	porque
725.	creer *(Crecer,* being more logical, is used in the annotated edition.)	creer.
729.	la luz se ve.	la luz se ve. *Vicente.* ¡Hado cruel!
758.	mi furor	me fuerza

	P	VT
771+.	*Escondese,* (Changed to: *Escóndense Don Vicente y Chocolate ...*)	*Escondese,*
782+.	No stage direction given.	No stage direction given.
817.	turbado *(Turbada,* being more logical, is used in the annotated edition.)	turbado
824+.	There is no stage direction.	*Sale Don Vicente.*
846.	su dolor.	tu rigor.
846+.	*hincase de rodillas, y Violante le detiene.*	*arrodillanse los dos, y detienele Violante.*
847.	*Violante.* puesta:	*Vicente:* puesto:
848.	dispuesta	dispuesto
851.	*Conde.*	*Vicente.*
853.	infelice	infeliz
874.	hoy	voy
881.	There is no stage direction.	*Vase.*
887.	lustre,	ilustre,
907.	que	cual
913.	el tercero el	el tercero
922.	empeñes	empeñas
926.	de veras,	veras

	P	VT
928+.	*Chocolate.* Cosas de tanta importancia se hablan mejor sin testigos. *Vase.*	Lines 928-929 are missing.
993.	mi	mi mi
997.	en	alli en
1038.	el deshacerle,	deshacerle,
1048.	¿Pues	Presto
1061.	imaginada,	teniendo imaginada,
1067.	el empeño	empeño
1068.	hallar de	hallarte
1087.	propias	prontas
1088.	con	en
1098.	hasta	basta
1101.	y porque a servirte	porque a ser tuya esta
1117.	y mi	mi
1126.	cielo,	cielos,
1141.	anticipado,	anticipada,
1142.	y	pues
1143.	te	me
1159.	dé yo parabienes de	yo dé parabienes a
1167.	tus	vuestros
1172.	la	lo
1174.	No me agradezcais,	No, no me agradezcais hoy,
1176.	que en el agrado que	en el agrado que hoy
1177+.	*Vase.*	*Vanse.*
1179.	Ya,	Si, ya,
1187.	alta region	region alta

	P	VT
1189.	a tales	tales
1199.	pretendia,	pretendias,
1206.	un	uno
1208.	se	le
1231.	cargando	cargado
1233.	hallarla,	hallarle,
1237.	empeño;	empleo;
1246.	imagino,	imaginas,
1252.	*Guillen.* Nuevo ha de ser el concepto.	*Guillen.* Nuevo ha se ser el concepto.
1253.	*Rey.* Dile.	Dile.
1298.	hubiera	hubiese
1316.	pueda	puede
1318.	a una	una
1339.	atrevi	me atrevi
1340.	adonde	adonde tu
1364+.	*Sale el Conde. Chocolate:* Yo he de entrar.	*Chocolate.* Yo he de entrar. *Sale el Conde.*
1365.	guste.	gustare
1373.	sois? Nadie.	sois vos? ¿Yo? Nadie.
1412.	que	pues
1429.	decirle, y no remediarle.	decirse, y no remediarse.
1432.	*Aparte.*	There is no stage direction.
1440.	ningun tiempo	tiempo alguno
1442.	asi yo	asi
1456.	yo	ya
1460.	yo	y no

	P	VT
1466+.	*muy triste Don Vicente.*	*Don Vicente muy triste.*
1475.	There is no stage direction.	*Aparte.*
1476.	*Aparte.*	There is no stage direction.
1498.	sea	se ha
1510.	hubo	que hubo
1518.	que	pues
1567.	para ti es,	es para ti,
1569+.	*Lea Vicente.*	*Vicente lee.*
1574.	*Aparte.*	There is no stage direction.
1576.	Este	Esta
1577.	le	la
1577+.	*Lea Vicente.*	*Vicente lee.*
1577d.	vais	vengais
1577f.	titulo	el titulo
1577g.	aquella	aquesta
1578.	*Vicente.* No es menor merced la mia;	*Violante.* ¿Qué escucho? *Vicente.* La merced mia no es menor;
1579.	dejadme penas, dejadme,	penas dejadme,
1580.	*Aparte.*	There is no stage direction.
1581.	There is no stage direction.	*Aparte.*
1609.	ningun medio.	medio ninguno.
1632.	pudiese, a que tu	pudiste a que, a su
1635.	en	con
1638.	Don Vicente	Vicente

	P	VT
1639.	This line is missing.	Noble eres, adios, Violante.
1639+.	*y salen*	*salen*
1652.	del	al
1653.	Dila.	Di.
1657.	le amaba,	se amaban,
1706+.	bajen a el. *Vase. Sale con manto.*	a el bajen. *Vase Elvira, y sale con manto Violante.*
1710.	O amiga, gana	Ya mi deseo
1715+.	(que hoy nacio, y ha muerto hoy).	This line is missing. Its inclusion disturbs the metric form of the *redondilla.*
1725.	aunque	que
1733.	ha	le ha
1734.	del Conde para	el Conde por mi
1735.	del Rey para	el Rey para su
1749.	que	hoy
1758.	hagas	hasta
1789.	conocer	merecer
1790.	There is no stage direction.	*Aparte.*
1799.	siempre contra si.	lo peor siempre.
1799+.	*y salen el Rey, y Don Guillen con capas de noche.*	*Salen el Rey, y Don Guillen en traje de noche.*
1802-1803.	These two lines are missing and are needed for the metric form of the *redondilla.*	porque, si algo nos sucede, sea facil encontrallo:

	P	VT
1809.	mas	de
1814.	This line is missing and is needed for the metric form of the *redondilla.*	*Rey.* En ocasion semejante,
1821.	altivo a	altivo
1854+.	*Tocan dentro.*	*Suenan dentro instrumentos.*
1861.	aliento.	acento.
1863+.	*a una ventana baja sale*	*sale a una reja baja*
1867.	de mi mi esposo,	mi esposo de mi,
1881.	viniese	viniere
1893.	que	que a
1897.	por	con
1900.	*Aparte.*	There is no stage direction.
1910.	esperais;	buscais;
1912.	porque	mas
1919.	This line is missing and is needed for the metric form of the *romance.*	porque no estaba aqui ayer.
1920.	dais,	me dais
1924.	la	y la
1928.	*Rey.* (Repeated unnecessarily.)	Omitted.
1929.	duda alguna	duda
1936.	o el	dél
1951+.	*y el Rey y Don*	*por un lado, y el Rey y*

	P	VT
	Guillen por otra parte.	*Don Guillen se retira por otro.*
1955.	no, no	no
1959.	There is no stage direction.	*Vase.*
1977.	alguno	uno
1978+.	*Vanse los dos, sale la Reyna a la misma ventana, y Elvira, y vuelven por otra parte, o puerta el Rey, y Don Guillen.*	*Vanse los dos, sale la Reyna a la misma ventana, y Elvira, y vuelven por otra parte, o puerta el Rey, y Don Guillen.*
2007.	della	dellas
2012.	cielos,	celos
2013.	el sentir, y el	de sentir, y
2015.	yo no	no yo
2016.	tuyo	suyo
2032.	hoy	una
2039.	gusto	justo el
2040.	estas	estais
2046.	adbitro	arbitrio
2047.	el	ese
2048.	reflejos	influjos
2058.	que los venza si,	vencer si, mas no
2059.	no	
2082.	fuera	fuese
2087+.	*Elvira*	*Llega Elvira*
2090.	fuerza	forzoso
2095+.	*Sale Chocolate.* (It is more logical that Guillén enter.)	There is no stage direction.

	P	VT
2096.	*Chocolate*	*Elvira.*
2108.	Juzgo que el hombre se va:	El hombre se va; de cuanto
2122.	basta	hasta
2129.	vas	vayas
2132.	*Rey.*	*Vicente.*
2140.	Labios	lauros
2141+.	*Salen*	*Sale*
2141+.	TERCERA JORNADA	JORNADA TERCERA
2146.	Dejate de la querella	deje ya que en tal porfia
2147.	del	al
2157.	lirio	lilio
2192.	continuado	continuando
2239.	Desconfianzas	Desconfianza
2242.	mayor?	y mayor?
2246.	ansi?	asi?
2249.	ha	he
2252.	por una carta	De Don Vicente
2253.	suya, que	que al campo
2256.	harto mi amor lo ha sentido.	que yo le tengo pedido:
2263.	de veros	deberos
2309.	ciego	vendado
2314.	*Guillen.*	*Dentro Guillen*
2315.	*Chocolate.*	*Dentro Chocolate.*
2317.	¡Caso fuerte!	¡Ese es caso fuerte!
2321+.	This line is missing and is needed for the metric form of the *romance.*	This line is missing and is needed for the metric form of the *romance.*

	P	VT
2326.	desaparecio.	se desaparece.
2333.	siguiendo	seguian
2334.	la	el
2351.	despues cuando	despreciando
2353.	huyen	huye
2360+.	*en el*	*del*
2371+.	These two lines are missing and are needed for the metric form of the *romance*.	*Rey.* Dime quien eres, o aqui hoy a morir te resuelve.
2374.	escojo	elijo
2376.	ostentar ser	ostentarte
2390.	es esta	esta es
2405.	Galasi	Galafre
2406.	a un	un
2411.	aqueste	este
2455.	aun	aun a
2456.	que	a que
2474.	ofenderte	ofrecerte
2484+.	*Vanse.*	*Vase el Rey y Don Guillen.*
2490.	les	lo
2501.	Yo soy. ¿Quien? Don Vicente.	Yo soy. ¿Quien? ¿No me conoces,
2502.	This line is missing and is needed for the metric form of the *romance*.	necio, que soy Don Vicente?
2504.	¿Donde	¿Adonde
2544.	Ten,	Tente,
2553.	me	ma

	P	VT
2567.	hubieras	hubiera
2590.	sin olvidarlo	mi discurso me
2592.	y yo	yo
2593.	fuga	fuga en
2594.	del	de
2599.	por mas	mas por
2605.	arbitro	arbitrio
2622.	quien soy; y ser	ser quien soy, y quien
2648.	*Vase.*	There is no stage direction.
2654.	Yo estoy	Estoy
2666.	particion	partición que
2669.	y uno	uno
2673.	personas	pasiones
2681.	habra para que, ni hube	habia para que no hubo
2683.	tenia	tenian
2687.	su	la
2694.	aqueste	a este
2695.	que no	cuando
2712.	ya	yo
2741.	no se	le
2742.	cuidado al	cuidadoso
2742+.	*Sale*	*Sale*
2743.	tu	su
2748.	Leonor	Leonora
2752.	un	un solo
2757.	amorosos *Abrazanse.*	amantes
2758.	There is no stage direction.	*Abrazanse.*
2763.	con	en
2769.	amante	amante y

	P	VT
2770.	he adelantado	adelanto
2775.	y me miras,	me miras,
2782.	traes	traes? di
2783.	*Aparte.*	There is no stage direction.
2784.	There is no stage direction.	*Aparte.*
2787.	queda	pueda
2788.	he imaginado mas de	imagino mas que
2794.	Y es lo peor que pudo	Lo peor es que pudiste
2797.	tiempo	tiempo a
2798.	venciera	vencieras
2801.	a Dios pluguiera.	pluguiera,
2803.	hasta	que hasta
2807.	*Aparte.*	There is no stage direction.
2808.	There is no stage direction.	*Aparte.*
2812.	y	que
2813.	Calle,	Bella
2821.	este	deste
2830.	¡Muerta vengo! ¿Que hay, Leonor? (The ending *-a* in *Leonora* is needed for the meter.)	¡Vengo muerta! ¿Qué hay, Leonor?
2831.	empiezas	concierta
2832.	Prosigue.	la voz. *Violante.* Di.

	P	VT
2834+.	Pues ¿y que sucedio? (This line is omitted in the annotated edition because it disturbs the metric form of the *romance.)*	This line is missing.
2835.	*Violante.* ¿Que ha sucedido?	*Vicente.* ¿Pues que ha sucedido? Que
2844.	tu	su
2865.	he	ha
2866.	nacio	necio
2879.	fui	he sido
2886.	no	no os
2892+.	*el*	*del*
2895.	está don Vicente adonde	esté Don Vicente donde
2896.	pueda	puedas
2902.	bella Violante	Violante hermosa
2903.	amor	de amor
2908.	cualquier	cualquiera
2915.	lo que hoy me arroja entrar,	la que hoy me arroja a entrar,
2916.	a que	aqui
2934.	mis	mas
2940.	*Aparte.*	There is no stage direction.
2941.	hablé?	hablé o
2946.	confesarla.	confirmarla.
2947.	penas!	pena!

	P	VT
	¡Ay mas desdichas!	¡Ay mas desdicha!
2951.	¡Ay (changed to *¿Hay* in the annotated edition.)	¡Ay
2952.	¡Ay (changed to *¿Hay* in the annotated edition.)	¡Ay
2974.	aquesta	aquella
2986.	ni ya	yo ni
2998.	y (changed in the text to comply with modern usage.)	y (changed in the text to comply with modern usage.)
2999.	su	tu
3014.	declinando vaya	declina y desmaya
3015.	ya el sol,	el sol ya,
3016.	a hacer	haré
3023.	guardarse	guardarle
3028.	*Aparte.*	There is no stage direction.
3030.	*Aparte.*	There is no stage direction.
3031.	There is no stage direction.	*Aparte.*
3037.	darele	la daré
3038+.	*la daga*	*con la daga*
3046.	Declarose	Dilatose
3049.	There is no stage direction. (Stage directions are	

	P	VT
	included in the annotated edition.)	There is no stage direction.
3060.	There is no stage direction. (Stage directions are included in the annotated edition.)	There is no stage direction.
3075.	pues que	porque
3080.	ha	he
3085.	y en	y
3092.	sin	con
3097.	jamas	la mas
3101.	no	uno
3103.	prevenga	prevengo
3123.	¡Ay mi	¡Ay
3130.	tenga	tengas
3145.	a ti	aqui
3169.	indignada	imputada
3189.	verdad es, que	verdad es,
3209.	yo	no
3212.	pero de culpada no.	y no de culpada yo.
3218.	es	el
3222.	vente *Vanse.*	ven aora
3222+.	*Salen apartados el Rey, y Don Vicente, el uno muy triste, y el otro muy alegre sin verse.*	*Vanse, y salen por distintos lados, sin verse el uno al otro, el Rey, y Don Vicente, uno muy triste, y otro muy alegre.*
3226.	el dia tras	tras el dia
3237.	persona.	persona dél.

	P	VT
3266+.	*sale*	*sale*
3280.	quisieran	quisieren
3282.	enemiga	enemigo
3294+.	*Seña*	*Suena*
3300.	esta vez ...	*Rey.* Esta vez ...
3300+.	Lleguen ... aparten	Lleguen ... aparten
3305.	Como	Como yo
3333.	abrazada	adorada
3357.	esa	esta
3386.	mis brazos dará el perdon;	mi abrazo os dará el perdon;
3401.	las plantas;	los pies,
3419.	ninguna	alguna
3424.	disgusto,	gusto,

NOTES TO THE TEXT

13. In the seventeenth century *soy* and *estoy* were used interchangeably.

36. In the Chronicle of Don Jaime, *Miravalle* appears as *Miravals;* in the *princeps* edition it appears as *Miraballe;* and in the Vera Tassis edition it is changed to *Miravalle.*

50-54. The allusion of *tres Pedros* seems to be to (1) Pedro I of Aragon (1074?-1104) King of Aragon and of Navarra who fought constantly against the Moors. (2) Pedro II of Aragon, I of Cataluña (1174-1213), called Pedro the Catholic. This Pedro is the one portrayed in this play. He was the son of Alfonso II and Doña Sancha of Castille. In 1196 this Pedro succeeded his father to the throne, and in 1204 he married Doña María of Montpellier. From this union was born James I the Conqueror. United with the Kings of Castille and Aragon, he fought against the *Almohades* in the battle of *Las Navas de Tolosa* 1212?). (3) Pedro III of Aragon, II of Cataluña, called Pedro the Great (1239-1285) was the son of Jaime I the Conqueror and of Violante of Hungary. Although Calderón does not adhere strictly to exact chronological sequence of historical events and borrows at random the names of true historical figures, the third Pedro alluded to could not have been born yet. The reference to the cruelty of the King in the play could not logically apply to Pedro I of Castille, called the Cruel and the Just for his irascible character and sanguinary vengeances. This Pedro also lived much later (1334-1369).

56. Archaic form of *hemos,* necessary here for the metric form of the *romance.*

58. In the seventeenth century the grammatical rule of *y* changing to *e* preceding the vowel *i* was not yet established. In the *princeps* edition *e* appears as *y.*

60. The paragogic *e* attached to *feliz (felice)* is needed here for the metric form of the *romance.*

67. This line was omitted from the *princeps* edition. Vera Tassis makes the correction, thus retaining the scheme of the *romance* in e-a.

76. In the seventeenth century the spelling of *ahora* still vacillated with *aora* and *agora.* All three forms are used interchangeably in the *princeps* and in the annotated editions.

81. It seems that *contarla* is a more logical word to use in this context. Vera Tassis makes the substitution from *soñarla.*

98. In the sixteenth and seventeenth centuries, feathers *(plumas)* signified adornment, pomp,

and magnificence; therefore, «lleno de plumas y lenguas» uttered by the Queen may be inferred to mean that Don Jaime, adorned in great splendor was being hailed *(lenguas)* for his virtues and great deeds.

129-132. It was typical in the Golden Age dramas for the *gracioso* to utter epigrams and witticisms. Often he gave advice to his master by employing unusual word play such as this one. Chocolate does this throughout the play.

143. Literally *tapaboca* is a blow which is given on the mouth with the palm of the hand or with the tip of the foil in fencing. Figuratively, it is any expression or action intended to cut off or suspend conversation, forcing one to keep quiet, especially when convinced that what is said is false.

151. *Acicate* is a Moorish spur used in horseback riding. It has a single iron point used to spur the horse. A small guard or tip is placed at a proportional distance to prevent undue penetration.

154. *Maleza* signifies weeds, underbrush, or thicket.

Intrincada is from *intrincar,* to entangle, complicate or confuse.

242. While *lustre* literally means luster or shine, figuratively it means splendor and glory.

248. In the sixteenth and seventeenth centuries, the spelling of the word *misma* still vacillated between *mesma* and *misma.*

270. An archaic form of *prisa.*

352. *Aqueste* and *aquesta,* archaic forms of *este* and *esta,* are used throughout the play in order to maintain the metric form of the verse.

359. *Declarar* in this context has the meaning of to make understand with clarity.

364. This is a play on words. *Llave maestra* is used figuratively in the sense that Don Vicente has a master key in the person of Leonor, the servant who gives him entrance to visit Violante. By this act, Leonor is actually betraying the trust of her master, Count Monforte.

365-366. The passage alludes to the fact that the King loves Violante while Count Monforte loathes Don Vicente.

371-374. Chololate's statement is far from being wrong. Many *comedias* of the Golden Age had honor and jealousy as a basic theme. Hymen Alpern has compiled a list of sixteenth and seventeenth century plays whose main theme is jealousy. See Hymen Alpern, «Jealousy as a Dramatic Motive in the Spanish Comedia», *Romanic Review,* XIV (1923), 276-285.

378-435. In this long passage, Chocolate discourses on a prevalent theme of Spanish literature since the middle ages—antifeminism. The most representative of this type of literature appeared in the second half of the fifteenth century and is known as *El Corbacho* or «Reprobación del amor mundano.» Alfonso Martínez de Toledo authored this work in four parts; the second part is dedicated to pointing out the defects of women. The biting satire against the vices of women makes this work the most important example in medieval misogynic literature.

465. *Ha* is used interchangeably with *hace* through-

out the play; this is in keeping with sixteenth and seventeenth century usage.

473. *Acuñar* has the meaning to coin money. The expression *Uno vela y otro acuña* infers that while some keep vigil (are on the lookout) others coin or mint money.

476. A *zángano* is a lazy man who lives off others. He is usually heavy, dull, and stupid. Etymologically, the word derives from the drone, the male species which distinguishes himself from the other bees by his thick body. He lives off the work of the laborers in the beehive.

477. *Medrar* is an archaic word, corrupted from the Latin verb *meliorare,* from *melior,* which means to improve and advance in some enterprise, health, or fortune.

478. *Tener de* plus infinitive was used interchangeably with *tener que,* the modern form; therefore, *tengo de servir* is equivalent to *tengo que servir.*

520. *Bizarría* is a composite of many adjectives. In its definition it encompasses many qualities peculiar to a man of high stature and good breeding: gallantry, valor, fortitude, liberality, generosity, splendor, and gentility. Since Count Monforte considers Don Vicente his arch enemy, he is loath to concede these prestigious qualities to him.

636-637. *Desmandar* means to stray from the flock; *querencia* applies to the tendency or inclination of man and of some animals to return to the original place where reared or raised or where they are accustomed to go. Thus, the passage is describing the stray beast making its way to the open meadow where it is accustomed to roam.

646. A study of the metric form employed in this part of the play makes it evident that a verse is missing following line 646. In order to complete the metric form of the *espinela* (a ten-line, octosyllabic stanza with the rhyme scheme abbaaccddc) a verse ending in *ida* needs to be inserted before the succeeding line.

712. The orthography of *oscuras* was not fixed in the language of the seventeenth century; thus, it alternates with the spelling *escuras*.

761. A *cancel* is a wooden screen. In ancient times it was also a glass window (probably opaque) behind which regal personages remained incognito in the royal chapel.

883. *Invicto* means not vanquished, always victorious.

925. Spanish dramatists have made use of *refranes* from the beginning of the Spanish theatre. What Calderón did was merely to follow the tradition in his plays. E. J. Gates feels that Calderón

> was apparently following the examples of Lope de Vega and Tirso de Molina, but his interest in proverbial lore must have been further stimulated by his five-year study at the University of Salamanca, center of proverb collecting during the first quarter of the Seventeenth Century.

See E. J. Gates, «Proverbs in the Plays of Calderón», *Romanic Review*, XXXVIII (1947), 203-215. Rodríguez Marín, in his collection of proverbs, offers several variations of this proverb: «Nunca viene una desgracia sola.» «Un mal llama a otro mal.» «Un mal otro trae detrás.» «Un mal sirve a otro de quicial.» See Francisco Rodríguez Marín, *Más de 21.000 refranes castellanos* (Madrid: Revista de Archivos, 1926), pp. 349, 498. Gonzalo Correas cites still another variation on the same theme: «Un mal no viene solo.» See Gonzalo Correas, *Vocabulario de refranes* (Madrid, 1924), p. 495.

997. Modern form, *al provisio*, meaning instantly, immediately.

1043. *Amancillado* carries the meaning of shamed, vanquished, from the verb *amancillar*, to stain one's good name and reputation.

1123. Rodríguez Marín offers a variation on this proverb: «A gran daño gran remedio.» See page 9 of his collection.

1139. It was an ancient custom for the vassal to request permission from his lord (in this instance, the King) to marry his daughters.

1164. The phoenix, a legendary bird, which according to ancient Egyptians was unique in its species: living five or six centuries, being consumed in fire by its own act, and being reborn from its own ashes.

1315-1318. Chocolate intends a pun here, inferring that hot chocolate is a common thing to enter a lady's bedroom in the morning. His entry into Violante's room, therefore, should not cause surprise since he, too, is called Chocolate.

1354-1355. The inference of this passage is that in matters of love, servants suffer the consequences of their master's folly, even though they are not responsible for their having fallen in love.

1454-1455. These verses allude to the same proverb cited in note 925.

1516. *Apurar* means to clarify and disentangle a matter so that there is no doubt or uncertainty as to its understanding.

1535. *Parangón* means a comparison of one thing and another.

1574-1575. Rodríguez Marín has included this proverb in his collection and offers several variations of it: «Viene envuelto el áspid en flores.» «So la linda yerba está la culebra.» «*Latet* anguis *in* herba.» See page 473 of his collection.

1577. The term *maestre de campo* was formerly used, denominating a high ranking official in the military who commanded a certain number of troops.

1580-1581. The word *cordel,* meaning a thin rope, implies the strong compulsion that Don Vicente feels to keep his anxiety a secret. He would figuratively choke his voice with the *cordel.*

1695. In Golden Age literature love was often alluded to by the phrase *el dios ciego.*

1807. *Presto* carries the meaning of right away, instantly, quickly.

1826. *Sin el día* signifies that night has fallen.

1872. *Terrero* carries the general meaning of terrace. More specifically, in the seventeenth century it applied to the place from which gentlemen courted their ladies in the palace.

1923. The modern rules on the orthographical variants of *primer (primero* and *primera)* had not been fixed in the language of the sixteenth and seventeenth centuries. The shortened form had to be employed here in order to conform to the eight syllable count of the *romance* ending in accented *é.* Similar use of the word is made in other verses.

2072. *Mondongo* is an archaic term of contempt attributed to a servant, as for example a kitchen wench. In the seventeenth century it applied specifically to a Queen's servant.

2097. *Red* in this context does not mean net, but rather the grille or grating in the window.

2132-2133. A pun is intended in the remark. *Acerado,* penetrating or sharp, with reference to a steel blade has no relationship to *cera,* wax. The similarity in spelling contrasting with the dissimilarity in meaning of the terms carries the force of the pun.

2138. *Querella* is equivalent to *queja,* complaint or quarrel. Thus, *dulce querella* may be interpreted as a lover's sweet lament.

2219. *Trocar* is equivalent to *cambiar por,* to exchange for. Thus, the King is saying that he was fortunate in exchanging the affliction with which he waited, for the glory he felt in seeing the Queen.

2226-2227. *Despique* means vengeance or revenge. The passage may be interpreted to mean: for if the vengeance for the hardship which you suffer has been to see the glory that you seek . . .

2246. Archaic form of *así.*

2248. *Tratar a* was equivalent to *tratar de* in seventeenth-century Spanish.

2260. *Brevemente* in this context has the meaning of shortly not briefly. The King, therefore, is saying that Don Vicente will be here shortly.

2264. *Albricias* is what is given to one bringing good news. A possible etymological explanation held by some is that *albricias* evolved from *albicias (alba,* white), since whoever came bearing the good news was dressed in white. On the contrary, one who bore sad tidings or condolences was draped in a black cloak symbolizing mourning.

2314. *Habéis de* is equivalent to *has de;* the long archaic form is needed here for the metric form.

2361. A *ribazo* is a sloping bank, a mound or a hillock.

2370. In the *princeps* edition there is an obvious omission following this line. Since Chocolate's utterance is a reply, it is logical to assume that the lines evoking such a response were in the preceding verses. Vera Tassis corrects the omission by inserting the King's effusion in verses 2371-2372.

2379-2380. The *gracioso* makes a pun in employing the terms *chocolate* and *cacao* (from which chocolate is derived). «Todo es cacao» carries the implication of being worthless, analogous to «Everything is worth a hill of beans.»

2385-2386. «Don Vicente para todos», refers to *Para todos,* book of miscellany by Juan Pérez de Montalbán, published in 1632. Reputedly, the fame of this work is attributed more to the comment which it occasioned rather than to its literary merits. Enemies censored, criticized, and ridiculed it with the same fervor that friends defended it. Among the most vehement censors was Francisco de Quevedo in his satirical poem, *Perinola.* The poem ends with these verses:

el licenciado libruno
dizen que por varios modos
hizo un libro para todos
no siendo para ninguno.
Al principio es importuno
a la postre es almanaque,
baturrilo y badulaque.
Y así suplico al poeta
que en el libro no me meta
y si me metió me saque.
Oh, doctor! tu para todos
entre el engrudo y la cola,
es juego de perinola
digno de otros mil apodos.
Pues en él, de varios modos,
para idiotas y gabachos
mezclas berzas con gazpachos.
Quítale el saca y el pon
y el deja, y será peón
para todos los muchachos.

Variations of the title, *Para todos,* appeared in succeeding publications. With malicious intent Matías de los Reyes published his book, *Para algunos,* in 1640. Later, Juan Fernández de Peralta offered another variation with his work, *Para sí,* published in 1661. (Information on this note was reported in: J. M. Osma, «Nota a *Gustos y disgustos son no más que imaginación*», *Hispania,* XX (1937), 47-54.

2390. From early times, seven has been a number considered to be highly important in literature as the most perfect, complete, and magical number.

2399. *Primero* in this context is employed as *antes.*

2402. *Postas* where post-houses or stage-houses stationed on roads at intervals of two or three leagues so that mail-men and other travelers could make their trips in relays, acquiring greater speed by exchanging mounts along the way.

2406. The reference in this verse is to *La puente de Mantible,* another play by Calderón, written in 1632.

2413. A *tahur is* a gambler or card shark. The term also carries the implication of being a thief as well as a gambler. The origin of the word is believed to be Arabic.

2425. *Algebrista* in former times was the term applied to a surgeon dedicated to restoring dislocated bones into place.

2427. The reference is to another of Calderón's plays, *Peor está que estaba,* written in 1640.

2436. *Billete* in this context means a brief letter.

2546-2548. Chocolate intends a pun with his remark, implying that servants are given to talk back to their masters.

2621. *Abono* carries the meaning of justification; thus, Don Vicente means that he is putting aside the alleged justification for his jealousy and is willing to admit that his imagination is responsible for his spiritual unrest.

2652. *Pendencia* is a quarrel or feud.

2859. Intending a denial of the accusation, Violante means to say: «No pasó ninguna vez.» Since the metric form restricts the use of words, the resulting line has an ambiguous meaning.

3068. By *media venganza* Don Vicente is referring to the fact that he is in a position to kill only

Violante. Since the other party to his supposed dishonor is of royal blood, he is unable to get satisfaction from him; the social code prevents him from taking up arms against the King.

3153. *Vía* is an archaic form of *veía*.

3367-3370. The *estribillo alludes to the proverb:* «Gustos y disgustos son sólo una leve imaginación.» See J. M. Sbarbi, *Diccionario de refranes, adagios, proverbios de la lengua española* (Madrid, 1922-1923).

3382. *Corrido* in this context means ashamed, abashed.

3415-3416. The two verses make reference to another proverb, also found in the collection of Rodríguez Marín. He cites a variation of this proverb: «Lo ajeno más que lo propio parece bueno.»

BIBLIOGRAPHY

ALONSO PEDRAZ, Martín. *Enciclopedia del idioma.* Madrid: Editorial Gredos, 1961.

ALPERN, Hymen. «Jealousy as a Dramatic Motive in the Spanish Comedia», *Romanic Review,* XIV (1923), 276-285.

ASHCOM, B. B. *A Descriptive Catalogue of the Spanish Comedias Sueltas in the Wayne State University Library and the Private Library of Professor B. B. Ashcom.* Detroit: Wayne State University Libraries, 1965.

ASTRANA MARÍN, Luis. *D. Pedro Calderón de la Barca. Obras completas (Dramas).* 3rd ed. Madrid: M. Aguilar, 1945.

BARRERA Y LEIRADO, Cayetano Alberto de la. *Catálogo bibliográfico y biográfico del teatro antiguo español.* Madrid: Rivadeneyra, 1860.

CABALLERO Y RUBIO, Ramón. *Diccionario de modismos de la lengua castellana.* 2nd ed. Buenos Aires: Librería del Ateneo, 1947.

CALDERÓN DE LA BARCA, Pedro. *Obras completas.* 2nd Ed. Ángel Valbuena Briones. Vol. II. Madrid: Aguilar, 1960.

CASTRO, Américo. «Algunas observaciones acerca del concepto del honor en los siglos XVI-XVII», *Revista de Filología Española,* III (1916), 21.

CHANDLER, Richard E., and SCHWARTZ, Kessel. *A new History of Spanish Literature.* Baton Rouge: Louisiana State University Press, 1961.

CIRLOT, Juan E. *A Dictionary of Symbols.* Trans. Jack Sage. London: Routledge and Kegan Paul, Ltd., 1962.

COE, Ada M. *Catálogo bibliográfico y crítico de las comedias anunciadas en los periódicos de Madrid desde 1661 hasta 1819.* Baltimore: Johns Hopkins Press, 1935.

CORREAS, Gonzalo. *Vocabulario de refranes y frases proverbiales (1626).* 2nd ed. Madrid: Tip. de la Revista de Archivos, 1924.

CORTÉS, Narciso Alonso. *El teatro en Valladolid.* Madrid: Tip. de la Revista de Archivos, 1923.

COTARELO Y MORI, Emilio. *Bibliografía de las controversias sobre la licitud del teatro en España.* Madrid: Tip. de la Revista de Archivos, 1914.

— —. *Catálogo de obras dramáticas impresas pero no conocidas hasta el presente con un apéndice sobre algunas piezas raras o no conocidas de los antiguos teatros francés e italiano.* Madrid: Marqués, 1902.

— —. *Catálogo descriptivo de la gran colección de comedias escogidas que consta de cuarenta y ocho volúmenes, impresos de 1652 a 1704.* Madrid: Tip. de Archivos, 1932.

— —. *Catálogo de una colección dramática española hasta fines del siglo XIX y de obras relativas al teatro español.* Madrid: Viuda e hijos de J. Rates, 1930.

— —. *Colección de entremeses, loas, bailes, jácaras, y mojigangas desde fines del siglo XVI a mediados del XVIII ordenados por Emilio Cotarelo y Mori.* Madrid: Bailly-Bailliere, 1911.

— —. *Ensayo sobre la vida y obras de D. Pedro Calderón de la Barca.* Madrid: Tip. de la Revista de Archivos, 1924.

— —. *Fonología española: pronunciación de los siglos XVI y XVII.* Madrid: Imprenta de la Revista de Archivos, 1909.

COVARRUBIAS HOROZCO, Sebastián de. *Tesoro de la lengua española; añadido por el padre Benito Remigio Noydens.* Madrid: Melchor Sánchez, 1674-75.

Cuadernos Bibliográficos, Cartelera teatral madrileña. Ed. Seminario de bibliografía hispánica de la Facultad de Filosofía y Letras de Madrid. Vol. I. Madrid: Consejo Superior de Investigaciones Científicas, 1961.

DESCLOT, Bernat. *Crónica.* Vol. II. Barcelona: Editorial Barcino, 1949.

Diccionario de la lengua castellana compuesto por la Real Academia Española. 3rd ed. Madrid: Viuda de J. Ibarra, 1791.

Diccionario de la lengua castellana en que se explican el verdadero sentido de las voces; compuesto por la Real Academia

Española. Autoridades. 6 vols. Madrid: Imprenta F. del Hierro, 1726-91.

FOLKARD, Richard. *Plant Lore, Legends, and Lyrics.* 2nd ed. London: Sampson Low, Marston and Company, Ltd., 1892.

FONTECHA, Carmen. *Glosario de voces comentadas en ediciones de textos clásicos.* Madrid: Consejo Superior de Investigaciones Científicas, 1941.

GATES, E. J. «A Tentative List of the Proverbs and Allusions in the Plays of Calderón», *PMLA,* LXIV (1949), 1027-1048.

— —. «Proverbs in the Plays of Calderón», *Romanic Review,* XXXVIII (1947), 203-215.

GUILLÉN DE CASTRO. *Obras de Don Guillén de Castro y Bellvis.* Ed. Eduardo Juliá Martínez. Vol. II. Madrid: Tip. de la Revista de Archivos, 1926.

HAYES, F. C. «The Use of Proverbs as Titles and Motives in the *Siglo de Oro* Drama: Calderón», *Hispanic Review,* XV (1947), 453-463.

HERDLER, A. W. «The Sentiment of Honor in Calderón's Theatre», *Modern Language Notes,* VIII (1893), 77-80.

HERRERO GARCÍA, Miguel. *Ideas de los españoles del siglo XVII.* Madrid: Editorial Voluntad, 1928.

HESSE, Everett W. *Calderón de la Barca.* New York: Twayne Publishers, Inc., 1967.

— —. «The Publication of Calderón's Plays in the Seventeenth Century», *Philological Quarterly,* XXVII (1948), 37-51.

HILBORN, Harry Warren. *A Chronology of the Plays of D. Pedro Calderón de la Barca.* Toronto: University of Toronto Press, 1938.

JONES, C. A. «Honor in Spanish Golden-Age Drama: Its Relation to Real Life and Morals», *Bulletin of Hispanic Studies,* XXXV (1958), 199-210.

MCCREADY, Warren T. *Bibliografía temática de estudios sobre el teatro español antiguo.* Toronto: University of Toronto Press, 1966.

MCKNIGHT, William A. *A Catalogue of Comedias Sueltas in the Library of the University of North Carolina.* Chapel Hill, 1965.

MEJÍA, Pedro. *Silva de varia lección.* Vol. II. Madrid: Sociedad de Bibliófilos Españoles, 1934.

MOLINARO, J. A., *et al.* *A Bibliography of Comedias Sueltas in the University of Toronto Library.* Toronto: University of Toronto Press, 1959.

MONTANER, Joaquín. *La colección teatral de don Arturo Sedó.* Barcelona: Seix y Barral, Hnos., 1951.

MUNTANER, Raimundo E. Bernardo Diesclot. *Cronache Catalane Del Secolo XIII e XIV.* Firenze, 1844.

OSMA, J. M. «Nota a *Gustos y disgustos son no más que imaginación*», *Hispania,* XX (1937), 47-54.

PALAU Y DULCET, Antonio. *Manual del libro hispanoamericano (1923-27).* 7 vols. 2nd ed. Vol. III. Barcelona, 1950.

PAZ Y MELIA, Antonio. *Catálogo de las piezas de teatro que se conservan en el departamento de manuscritos de la Biblioteca Nacional.* 2nd ed. Madrid: Blass, 1934.

PÉREZ PASTOR, Cristóbal. *Documentos para la biografía de D. Pedro Calderón de la Barca.* Madrid: Tip. de Fortanet, 1905.

— —. *Memorias de la Real Academia Española.* Vol. X. Madrid: Hijos de Reus, 1910.

— —. *Nuevos datos acerca del histrionismo español de los siglos XVI y XVII.* Madrid, 1901.

PERRY, Janet H., ed. *The Heath Anthology of Spanish Poetry.* Boston: D. C. Heath and Company, 1954.

PFANDL, Ludwig. *Historia de la literatura nacional española en la edad de oro.* Trans. José Rubio Balaguer. Barcelona: Sucesores de Juan Gil, 1933.

RODRÍGUEZ MARÍN, Francisco. *Más de 21.000 refranes castellanos.* Madrid: Revista de Archivos, 1926.

RODRÍGUEZ MOÑINO, Antonio R. *Catálogo de los manuscritos poéticos castellanos existentes en la Biblioteca de The Hispanic Society of America.* New York: Hispanic Society of America, 1965-66.

ROGERS, Paul Patrick. *The Spanish Drama Collection in the Oberlin College Library; A Descriptive Catalogue.* Oberlin, 1940.

SALVÁ Y MALLÉN, Pedro. *Catálogo de la Biblioteca de Salvá.* Vol. I. Valencia: Imprenta de Ferrer de Orga, 1872.

SÁNCHEZ ARJONA, José. *Noticias referentes a los anales del teatro en Sevilla.* Sevilla: E. Rasco, 1898.

SBARBI, J. M. *Diccionario de refranes, adagios, proverbios de la lengua española.* Madrid, 1922-23.

SCHACK, Adolfo Federico de. *Historia de la literatura y del arte dramáticos en España.* Trans. Eduardo Mier. Vols. IV and V. Madrid: M. Tello, 1887.

SEPÚLVEDA, Ricardo. *El corral de la Pacheca.* Madrid: Fernando Fe, 1888.

SIMÓN DÍAZ, José. *Bibliografía de la literatura hispánica.* 6 vols. Madrid: Consejo Superior de Investigaciones Científicas, 1950-1962.

SLOMAN, A. E. *The Dramatic Craftsmanship of Calderón.* Oxford: The Dolphin Book, 1958.

STUART, D. C. «Honor in the Spanish Drama», *Romanic Review,* I (1910), 247-258, 357-366.

TICKNOR, George. *History of Spanish Literature.* Vol. II. 4th ed. New York: Harper and Bros., 1891.

TIMONEDA, Juan. *Rosas de romances (1573).* Valencia: Editorial Castalia, 1963.

VEGA CARPIO, Lope Félix de. *Obras de Lope de Vega.* Ed. Marcelino Menéndez y Pelayo. Vol. 8. Madrid: Sucesores de Rivadeneyra, 1898.

— —. *Obras escogidas.* Ed. Federico Carlos Sainz de Robles. Vol. II. Madrid: M. Aguilar, 1946.

WHITNEY, James Lyman. *Catalogue of the Spanish Library; Bequeathed by George Ticknor to the Boston Public Library.* Boston: Library Trustees, 1879.

WILSON, Edward M. «The Four Elements in the Imagery of Calderón», *Modern Language Review,* XXXI (1936), 34-37.

ZURITA, Gerónimo. *Anales de la Corona de Aragón.* Vol. I. Zaragoza: Diego Dormer, 1469.

Simón Díaz, José. *Bibliografía de la literatura hispánica.* 6 vols. Madrid: Consejo Superior de Investigaciones Científicas, 1950-1962.

Sloman, A. E. *The Dramatic Craftsmanship of Calderón.* Oxford: The Dolphin Book, 1958.

Stuart, D. C. «Honor in the Spanish Drama». *Romanic Review* I (1910), 247-258, 357-366.

Ticknor, George. *History of Spanish Literature.* Vol. II. 4th ed. New York: Harper and Bros. 1891.

Timoneda, Juan. *Rosas de romances (1573).* Valencia: Editorial Castalia, 1963.

Vega Carpio, Lope Félix de. *Obras de Lope de Vega.* Ed. Marcelino Menéndez y Pelayo. Vol. 6. Madrid: Sucesores de Rivadeneyra, 1895.

—, *Obras escogidas.* Ed. Federico Carlos Sainz de Robles. Vol. II. Madrid: M. Aguilar, 1946.

Whitney, James Lyman. *Catalogue of the Spanish Library Bequeathed by George Ticknor to the Boston Public Library.* Boston: Library Trustees, 1879.

Wilson, Edward M. «The Four Elements in the Imagery of Calderón». *Modern Language Review,* XXXI (1936), 34-47.

Zurita, Jerónimo. *Anales de la Corona de Aragón.* Vol. I. Zaragoza: Diego Dormer, 1669.